The World of
Model Aircraft

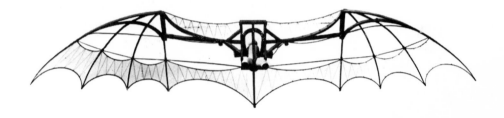

Companion volumes by Guy R. Williams

In preparation
The World of Model Cars

Already published
**The World of Model Trains
The World of Model Ships and Boats**

The World of
Model Aircraft

Guy R. Williams

André Deutsch
in association with Rainbird Reference Books.

This book was designed and produced by
Rainbird Reference Books Limited,
Marble Arch House, 44 Edgware Road, London, W2,
for André Deutsch Limited
105 Great Russell Street London WC1B 3LJ

House Editor: Peter Coxhead
Designer: Michael S. Lloyd

First published 1973
© Guy R. Williams 1973

The text was set in Monophoto Imprint 11/13 by
Jolly and Barber Limited, Rugby, England
The book was printed and bound by
Dai Nippon Printing Company Limited,
Tokyo, Japan

ISBN: 0 233 96286 7

PRINTED IN JAPAN

Contents

List of Colour Plates

Acknowledgments

No book of this kind, dealing with so wide-ranging a subject, could be compiled without much assistance from the recognized authorities. Among those to whom I am especially grateful are the following people and companies who have contributed significantly to the material contained in the book, or who have most generously given information or advice, or have helped in other ways. Nevertheless, full editorial responsibility for the text and for the captions to the pictures is my own.

Argentina

Gerardo Petrocella, Secretary of Technical Centre, Fédération Argentine D'Aero-Modelisme.
Eliseo Scotto, Director of Technical Centre, Fédération Argentine D'Aero-Modelisme.

Canada

Captain A. F. Christoffersen, Victoria, B.C.
Percy Grondin: Editor, *Canadian Model Aircraft*.
Dave Henshaw: Late President, Model Aeronautics Association of Canada.
W. P. Paris: Secretary General, Royal Canadian Flying Clubs Association.

Germany

Johannes Graupner: Kirchheim-Teck.

Great Britain

David Burrage: Insight Public Relations Limited.
M. A. L. Coote: Ripmax Limited.
E. F. H. Cosh: General Manager, E. Keil and Company Limited.
Chris Ellis: Editor, *Airfix Magazine*
Keith J. Harris: Antique Model Aeroplane Society.
A. A. Judge: Experimental Department, Mobo Toys.
P. S. Leaman: Membership Secretary, Cross and Cockade (Great Britain).
R. G. Moulton: Editor, *Aero Modeller*
Ian S. Peacock: Public Relations Officer, Society of Model Aeronautical Engineers.
Leslie A. Rogers: Secretary, Cross and Cockade (Great Britain).
Colin Sparrow: 'Beatties of London'.

Israel

Avner Mandelman: Chief Instructor, Aeromodelling Department, The Aero-Club of Israel.

New Zealand

John Malkin, Upper Hutt.
W. J. Parsons: Secretary, Royal New Zealand Aero Clubs, Inc.

United States of America

John Clemens: President, Academy of Model Aeronautics.
Michael Cullis: Assistant Manager, Advertising and Public Relations, Revell, Inc.
Annie Gieskieng: National Free Flight Society.
M. W. Gieskieng Jr.: Former Editor, *National Free Flight Society Digest*.
Carl Goldberg: Carl Goldberg Models, Inc.
Carl Kratzer: Former Editor, *Model Rocketeer*
Bill Ladner: President, Society of Antique Modelers.
Elaine Sadowski: Editor, *Model Rocketeer*.
Edward C. Sweeney Jr.: Editor, *American Aircraft Modeler*.
John Worth: Executive Director, Academy of Model Aeronautics.

1 The World of Model Aircraft

A buzz that sounds like the noise made by a thousand frenzied bluetail flies trying to escape from a jam jar may occasionally disturb the public peace in any relatively civilized part of the world. Tracked to its source, the din will probably be found to come from a miniature airfield, populated by a number of men and boys who are flying their miniature airplanes. There may be women and girls there too, but they are likely to be in a minority.

The enthusiasts, standing singly or in groups on and near the field, will almost certainly be drawn from all walks of life – it is quite possible that wealthy industrialists, comfortably-off professional men, artisans, students and school children, whose weekly spending-money is barely sufficient to cover the expenses of their hobby, will be there. The models on view will be just as mixed – there will probably be a number of small hand-launched gliders there, each of which will have cost less than a loaf of bread, and they may well be sharing the air with some highly sophisticated radio-controlled models in which has been invested a large part of their owners' years' earnings.

Everyone present will be enjoying himself hugely, for aeromodelling is an activity with an almost universal appeal. It pleases the young – almost as soon as a child is able to walk, it will watch its more accomplished companions make paper airplanes that glide smoothly across the playspace, and will try to learn this particular skill. By the time he is eight, a young man may well be taking part in important contests actually intended for his seniors (Ken Crammy, aged exactly that, flew his first big powered model plane in the 1971 United States Free Flight Championships held at Taft, California). Aeromodelling appeals, too, to the not-so-young. One grandfather, for example, competes regularly at the United States Model Aircraft Championships and tries never to miss an important meet.

To understand the popularity of aeromodelling today, we must firstly examine the various types of models.

Many different types of aircraft are encountered in model form, but they can be roughly allocated to three principal categories –

1 Part of a diorama showing the world's first powered flight – near Kitty Hawk in 1903

there are model airplanes (or aeroplanes), model flying boats and seaplanes (described most specifically in Chapter 5) and model rockets (described in Chapter 13). A fourth category might be added, to include model airships and balloons, but these do not seem, as this book is being prepared, to arouse as much enthusiasm as models of the other types.

Whichever of the above categories it falls in, a model aircraft may be regarded as either static or operational (though a flying model may be judged on its appearance when it is at rest on the ground, or on water). If a model is not expected to fly, it can be made from materials that do not have to conform so exactly to requirements of weight or strength. Many of the finest static models are made for display purposes by, or on behalf of, manufacturers of real aircraft, proprietors of air lines, or the military services. Experimental models designed for use in wind tunnels could, at a pinch, be called both 'static' and 'operational'.

As will be seen from Chapter 3 and other chapters, there are many different ways in which model aircraft can be constructed, but all the models can be divided, again, into two more general categories – those made professionally, to fulfil some specific purpose, usually for display or testing, or those intended for personal enjoyment. The latter may be sub-divided into those that

2 Below – A museum model of an Avro *Lancaster* bomber Mark 1

3 Right – A model, produced for publicity purposes, of the Anglo-French *Concorde*

4 Right below – A scale model of the YC-97A Stratofreighter undergoing a test in the Boeing wind tunnel

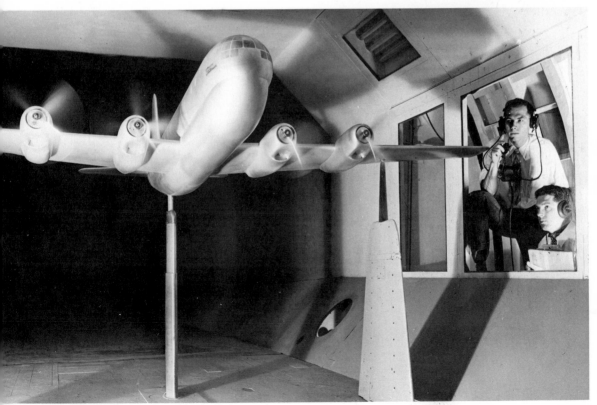

Left – Dennis Bronco's A/2 Nordic towline glider, designed by the famous hand-launch glider expert Lee Hines. Dennis was a member of the U.S. team that took part in the 1971 World Championships.

Right – A catapult-launched model glider

Below – An original model of the 'Flying Carriage', built by Alberto Santos-Dumont in 1899–1900

are made on a 'scratch' or amateur basis, and those that are purchased ready-made, or in kit form (described in Chapter 12).

So many different materials can be used today for making model
aircraft that it is impossible to use these as a basis for model
classification. There are paper models, wooden models, metal
models and plastic models, but relatively few are constructed of
one of these materials alone. And, new materials are constantly
being brought into use as the manufacture of synthetics becomes
increasingly sophisticated. It is safer, then, to allot a model to one
of the following less controversial categories:

Made exactly to scale
Made approximately to scale
Not intended to resemble a real aircraft in any appreciable way.

Models falling in the third of these categories are usually
intended to operate as efficiently as possible and thus their appearance is entirely subordinated to this function.

There are several different ways in which model aircraft can be
made to move:

They may be gliders or soarers – launched, possibly, by hand,
or by some form of catapult, or by a towline. (In the latter case,
a cord is looped round a metal hook fixed to the underside of the
fuselage. When the operator moves forward, as swiftly as
possible, the glider or sailplane also moves forward, and upwards.
As soon as it has reached the required altitude, the towline falls
away, and the model travels on independently.) True model
gliders and soarers do not rely on any form of mechanical power
once they are satisfactorily airborne.

They may be rubber-powered (see Chapter 4).

They may be powered by one or more internal combustion
engines driving one or more propellers. Several different types
of these are made. They are described in Chapter 7.

They may be powered by one or more engines of the 'jet' or
'rocket' type. Fuller information about these models is given in
Chapters 8 and 13.

8 Above – Dennis Jaecks with a
'Pennyplane' model. Intended for
indoor competitions, these models
must weigh as much as a U.S.
penny (3 grams) and are limited
to an 18 in wingspan and length.

9 Right above – A radio-
controlled model of a flying boat

10 Right – A rubber-powered
model of a Bristol fighter made
from a pre-World War II Comet
kit

An increasing number of aeromodellers have been turning their
attention, in recent years, to the design and construction of
miniature helicopters. These little aircraft, which can rise and
descend vertically by means of overhead power-driven rotor blades,
are admirably suited for indoor flying, as, being so easily manoeuvr-
able, they can make the best possible use of a limited space.

Once model aircraft have started to move, they may be directly
answerable to the instructions of a 'pilot' on the ground, or they

11 An outdoor gas-powered
free-flight scale model, built and
flown by Darrin Mathews, which
won its event at the 1972
American Nationals

may be required to fly freely and independently, answering in this latter case only to some built-in form of control. 'Free flight' model aircraft are discussed in Chapter 11.

Model aircraft that remain, even when airborne, under ground control can be divided into two principal categories:

Those that are tethered to some form of control line or lines. (These are described in Chapter 9.)
Those that are controlled by radio (see Chapter 10).

In recent years, the hobby – or sport, or study, or whatever you like to call it – has changed its image considerably. Now, junior aeromodellers aim to become senior aeromodellers just as quickly as they can. Senior aeromodellers try to live down the fallacious legend that they are just a bunch of irresponsible adolescents playing with the toys they have nearly outgrown. So, at any representative meet, problems of advanced engineering and of aerodynamics will be discussed learnedly by all members of the assembled company, whatever their individual ages. To understand why popular aeromodelling 'grew up' suddenly, one has to know a little about the economic background against which most of the world's great controlling bodies matured.

In the United States, for instance, great interest was taken in model aviation in the years immediately prior to World War 2. After this war, when air travel was clearly going to become a major factor in global affairs, this interest increased a hundredfold. Aeromodelling was fostered in America, to a large extent, by various

12 Fulton Hungerford's fine flying scale model of a Ford Trimotor

organizations such as the American Legion and the National Exchange Club, both of which sponsored a number of exciting competitive events. The late forties and fifties saw the great Air Youth Meets sponsored by the Plymouth Corporation, more than a decade of National Model Airplane Championships at which the United States Navy acted as hosts, fourteen years of Payload and Cargo Competitions sponsored by Pan American Airways, and the Air Youth State Championships sponsored by the Hobby Industry Association of America. Outstandingly successful in popularizing competitive model flying were the Free Flight World Championships held at Suffolk County Air Force Base on Long Island, New York, in 1954, which were sponsored by the Convair Division of General Dynamics. The prizes offered in this great promotional bonanza were inviting. Real airplanes were awarded to the lucky winners of the principal contests at some of the biggest newspaper-financed meets.

With all this aeromodelling activity in the United States, the growth of the national controlling body – the Academy of Model Aeronautics (AMA) – was rapid. Its headquarters are located in Washington, D.C. Some historians believe that the movement for an organization like the Academy began as early as 1932. It was fostered carefully and without thought of personal gain by a Lieutenant H. W. Alden, whose home was in Ridgefield, New Jersey. Alden had been active for some years setting up model clubs and arranging contests, paying the heavy correspondence costs and most of his fares out of his own pocket. Ernest A. Walen, model expert and club leader from Springfield, Massachusetts,

13 Left — A control-line model of a Supermarine *Spitfire*

14 Below — A radio-controlled scale model of a Nieuport fighter

wrote from his personal experience of this dedicated innovator:

'I usually try to spend an evening with Lt Alden when possible. My respect and sincere liking for him increases as time goes on. . . We have Lt Alden to thank for the undoubted fact that model aviation is becoming an increasingly worth-while and dignified sport and hobby instead of a mere child's plaything . . .'

Certainly, in 1932, Lt Alden started, with William R. Enyart, the Junior Membership plan of the National Aeronautic Association (NAA). One year later a 'National' meet was held at Long Island, but proceedings were not entirely harmonious. A reliable observer recorded:

'There was too much petty strife, and there was no body (or organization) to which the modellers could be referred for discussions . . .'

The year after that, another 'National' meet was held at Akron, Ohio, under the joint sponsorship of the Akron Men's Chapter of the NAA, the Akron Women's Chapter of the same organization, the Akron Chamber of Commerce and the *Universal Model Airplane News*. At these early meets, it was customary for a 'technical symposium' to be held on the morning after all the competitions had been successfully completed. (Many contestants, physically and nervously exhausted by the exertions of the past few days, slept peacefully through these earnest gatherings, but no matter.) At the Akron winding-up session in 1934 the delegates who managed to keep awake favoured the idea of a separate organization being formed, to be run 'of, by and for' the model airplane builders of the nation. Established on a very small scale in 1936, the Academy grew and grew until, by 1960, its estimated membership was over 22,000. By that time, however, the great days of almost unlimited sponsorship were over. No longer were so many major industrial undertakings ready to part with their cash to finance lavish aeromodelling events unless they could see some really tangible returns. After a brief period without much of its accustomed outside financial help, the academy was practically faced with bankruptcy.

Then, in this crisis, some of the academy's most astute executives saw, suddenly and clearly, that aeromodelling, which had previously been thought of, primarily, as a youth activity, had become something quite different from that which it had been. Its principal appeal by this time, they saw, was to adults – even to very mature and prosperous men. Some radical changes in the academy's policy followed, and as a result the academy today has a membership of at least 40,000, some very adequately paid officials, and the responsibility of sanctioning more than seven hundred

model airplane annual contests throughout the country. It maintains official performance records for all competitions held in the United States. And it conducts the National Model Airplane Championships, which serve as a yearly measure of progress in modelling.

Many months of advance preparation are called for by this event. Almost 2,000 contestants converged on the Glenview Naval Air Station, Illinois, for the 1971 meet. They were assisted by more than 400 mechanics, and between them they won over 500 trophies and awards – provided, largely, by the contributions of more than 40 public companies and organizations that depend for their success on the popularity of aeromodelling. One hundred and twenty AMA officials were needed to supervise the events and the smooth running of the proceedings was aided by more than 300 able and cordial naval air-station personnel (150 of these state-remunerated hosts were assigned directly to the contest areas. The rest helped to control traffic and to perform other onerous but necessary duties.) In 1972, the Navy was able to provide more limited sponsorship.

The AMA is the only organization which may direct American participation in international aeromodelling. As early as 1953 the USAF flew Russ Nichols, Executive Director of the AMA to Holland,

15 An early model of a helicopter

so that he could represent American modellers at the meeting of the 'Fédération Aéronautique Internationale' (FAI) at which rules for the new World Championships were to be established. Soon globally-minded aeromodellers were travelling thousands of miles in their determined attempts to win a little glory for their homelands – and, incidentally perhaps, a little for themselves. And, the host countries met the occasion. The Radio Control Aerobatics World Championships, planned to take place at the Central Bucks County Airport, Doylestown, Pennsylvania, were renamed, by a proclamation issued by the Governor of the Commonwealth of Pennsylvania, 'International Radio Control Week'. 'This was possibly a once-in-a-lifetime opportunity to see the world's best modellers', said *Model Aviation*, official organ of the AMA. Everyone who could, should plan on attending. They would see teams from Australia, Austria, Belgium, Canada, Denmark, England, Finland, France, Germany, Ireland, Italy, Japan, Korea, Liechtenstein, Luxembourg, the Netherlands, Norway, South Africa, Spain, Sweden, Switzerland and the United States.

Yes, aeromodelling's growth rate in other countries has almost kept pace with that of America.

The controlling body in Great Britain – the Society of Model Aeronautical Engineers (SMAE) – which was originally founded in

16 A model of Boeing Fortress I made from an Airfix plastic kit of a Fortress II and modified during assembly

the early 1900s to promote model kite and balloon flying, now has more than a hundred smaller clubs affiliated to it, and there are equally active representative bodies in most of the other countries of the world. The FAI working from its base in Paris keeps a gently fostering eye over all.

In Israel – to examine the situation in one lively Middle Eastern country – aeromodelling is popular today with young and old alike, and the activities of more than ten thousand enthusiasts are carefully watched over by the country's Aero Club. This club was founded shortly before World War 2, and its first members experimented with primitive man-carrying gliders. These gliders, made in Poland, were launched from hill-tops, and after their flights were over, they were pulled uphill again by mules and camels. The club now has members in almost every city, town and village in the land.

The 'generation gap', said to be so evident in the Western democracies, is almost impossible to detect in Israeli aeromodelling circles. 'One of the nicest things about the Aero Club of Israel is the friendliness and lack of formality among its members', reports Avner Mandelman, a senior official. To emphasize his point, he records that during the national competitions, officers of very high rank in the Israeli Air Force, who are themselves modellers, cheerfully lend their equipment to, or swop equipment with, modellers who are not yet even fifteen years old. 'The competitions have the air of big picnics', Mandelman concludes. These happy Israeli get-togethers are held, as far as possible, during such public holidays as 'Succoth' or 'Passover', so that as many people as possible can join in the fun without having to miss either work or school.

Most aeromodellers – in whatever part of the world they are operating – will be helped in their technical researches by at least one of the many magazines and journals that are published specially for them. In America, the *American Aircraft Modeler* comes monthly from the Potomac Aviation Publications, and the *Junior American Modeler*, as its name implies, is intended principally for beginners and youth. In Britain, the *Aero Modeller* provides up-to-date information; in Brazil, *Sport Modelismo* is read; in Denmark, *Flyv*; in France, *Le Modele Reduit D'Avion* and *Radio Modelisme*; in India, *Indian Modeller*; in Italy, *Modelli e Sport* and *Modellismo*; in Japan, *Koku Fan*; in the Netherlands, *Modellen Revue*; in Spain, *Flaps*; in West Germany, *Flug Modell-Technik* and *Flug Revue*; and there are many more in these and other countries. It would be difficult to compile an up-to-date and comprehensive list as so many hobby magazines have an ephemeral existence. If one magazine in the aeromodelling world fades away, however, it is almost certain to be replaced by at least one other magazine.

Not all the devotees present at an aeromodellers' rally will

17 A model rocket that carries a camera in its nose cone. It is capable of taking super-8mm motion pictures during flight.

necessarily be aware of the good they are doing. 'Although model aircraft building and flying have changed with the times, the educational benefits derived are needed more than ever in today's society', claimed the officials of America's Academy of Model Aeronautics in a recent publication. 'Through model building, youngsters learn problem solving and the application of knowledge. Comprehension, patience, dexterity, the rewards of progress and the satisfaction of completion are dominant. Through model flying, applied scientific principles are learned, as well as judgment and sportsmanship.' Charles D. Lancaster of British Columbia, writing to Dave Henshaw, President of the Model Aeronautics Association of Canada (MAAC) and to Percy A. Grondin, Editor of *Canadian Model Aircraft*, the official journal of the MAAC, stated the same proposition in more urgent terms:

'. . . I am absolutely appalled when I find that so many communities of 5,000 people or over do not have any control line club or flying. This is very wrong. No wonder that we have a drug problem and a youth problem. Where are we[?]. What about the adults in our midst who are dying to learn about R/C [Radio-controlled flying] and do not know where to turn and when some friendly R/C'er sucks them in with obsolete used gear. We are missing so very many new and good people. . . . This Canada of ours should be a leader in this game, we can get anything we need from anywhere and we have the people who can do anything. Why, for God's sake, don't we use the potential that is put before us before it is too late . . .'

This hobby, which fulfils so many useful social purposes and promotes friendships between members of all classes and age groups, has not a very long history. Let us go on, now, to make a short survey of the models constructed in its very earliest days.

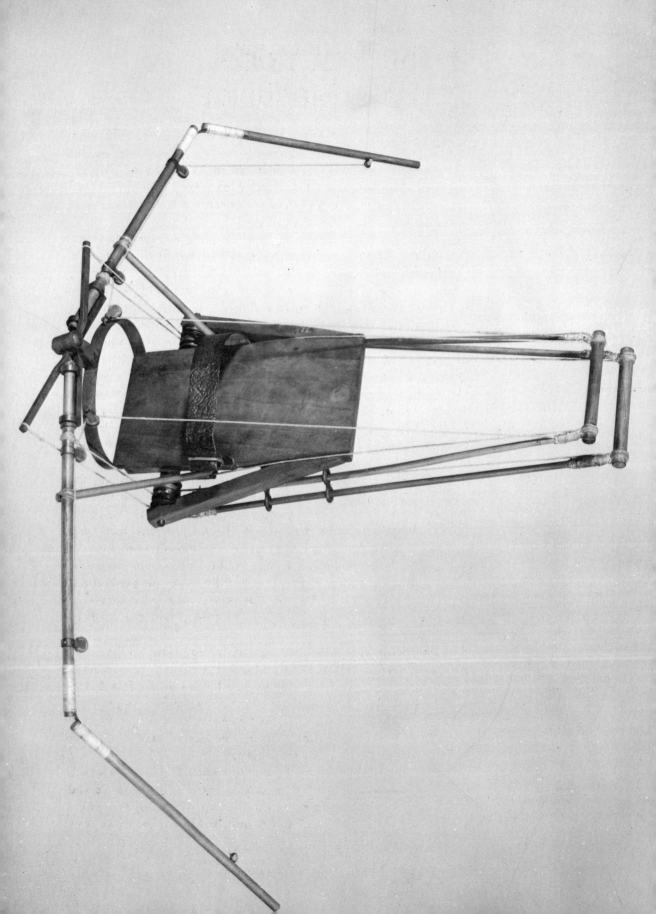

2 The First Model Flying Machines

' . . . There are three things which are too wonderful
for me, yea, four which I know not :
The way of an Eagle in the air . . .'

These words from the Book of Proverbs were written more than two thousand years ago, and they express brilliantly man's age-old yearning for adventure in the skies – a yearning that led many primitive people, a little more adventurous than their fellows, to jump off the tops of high rocks and other elevated places, hoping that rapid movements of their arms would keep them aloft. All crashed, of course, and many died, and eventually it became clear that wings of some kind would be necessary if air travel, for humans, was to be a practical proposition.

So, wings or substitutes for wings were made – crude appendages constructed usually of wood and feathers – but no one managed to remain airborne with them for more than two or three frantic seconds except a Frenchman, M. Besnier. Besnier is said to have attached to his shoulders two rods which had, at their extremities, hinged surfaces that closed on the upstroke and opened on the downstroke. With these accessories, Besnier is believed to have flapped his way successfully from one bank of a river to the other. Later adventurers who have tried to emulate this feat have finished their flights consistently and ignominiously in disaster.

It is tempting to believe that Man would not have conquered the air as soon as he did, if a few exceptionally clever people had not thought of trying out, on a miniature scale, their ideas for flying machines. In these early researches, we may find the birth of aeromodelling.

Leonardo da Vinci – scientist, engineer and painter of the *Mona Lisa*, the *Virgin of the Rocks*, and other masterpieces – was certainly among the first of these distinguished innovators. His extraordinarily interesting designs for winged flying apparatus and for a helicopter, together with some acute observations on the flight of birds, are to be found in the famous collection of his manuscripts now in the Ambrosian Library at Milan.

It is unlikely that any of Leonardo's winged machines would ever have flown successfully, for he based them on the age-old and erroneous assumption that if a man is to achieve flight he must somehow imitate a bird as closely as possible. It is known, however,

8 A museum model of an ornithopter (a flap-wing machine) after a design by Leonardo da Vinci (1452–1519)

9 Left – The Christ Child with 'whirligig' toy (detail from a 15th century panel picture in the Musée du Mans, Le Mans)

10 Top – A wind-mill toy or model helicopter model shown as a marginal illustration in a 14th century Flemish psalter

11 Above – A museum model of a spring-driven helicopter made from a drawing by da Vinci

that Leonardo designed and constructed several small spring-driven models based on helical screws that rose spectacularly into the air. Charles H. Gibbs-Smith has pointed out that da Vinci obtained the idea for these elementary but important models from Chinese tops that had found their way into Europe across the Middle Eastern trade routes many years before, or from the children's 'whirligig' toys that had been based on these. These is a painting in the Museum at Le Mans, in France, dating from about 1460, in which the Christ child is shown standing on the lap of the Virgin Mary with one of these toys in his hand. A similar toy was shown in a stained glass window of a little later date, which was formerly in the church at Stoke Poges, in Buckinghamshire, England, but cannot now be traced.

Two centuries, more or less exactly, after Leonardo da Vinci was born, Robert Hooke, who was a brilliant pupil at Westminster School under Doctor Busby, claimed that he had invented 'thirty several ways of flying'. In the year 1655, when he was twenty years old, Hooke made some notes which testify to the fact that he had not only dealt at length with the theory of the subject, but had actually:

'Contriv'd and made many Trials about the Art of flying in the air, and moving very swift on Land and Water, of which I shew'd several Designs to Dr Wilkins then Warden of Wadham College, and at the same time made a Module [model] which, by the help of Springs and Wings, rais'd and sustain'd itself in the Air; but finding by my own trials, and afterwards by calculation, that the Muscles of a Man's Body were not sufficient to do anything considerable of that kind, I apply'd my Mind to contrive a way to make artificial Muscles; divers designs whereof I shew'd also at the same time to Dr Wilkins, but was in many of my Trials frustrated of my expectations. . . .'

During the eighteenth century, men managed to ascend successfully and safely into the sky for the first time – only, they did this by means of lighter-than-air balloons. It was an English baronet – Sir George Cayley – who, between the years 1799 and 1809, pushed aeronautical research with heavier-than-air machines a few significant stages further. Cayley, like da Vinci, carried out most of his preliminary experiments with models. In the course of his studies, Cayley established for the first time the modern configuration of an airplane, consisting of a body (now called, usually, a 'fuselage'), main wings, a tail unit and an undercarriage. He discovered the value of curved or cambered surfaces in generating 'lift' (the force that keeps an aircraft aloft). He found out how horizontal and vertical surfaces could be manipulated to control a plane. And, he discovered that the upturning of wings – referred to, after this, as 'dihedral' – helped to produce lateral stability. With prophetic insight, he appears to have foreseen the ultimate development of the internal combustion engine. His classic paper *On Aerial Navigation*, published in 1809–10, gave a start to all our present-day knowledge of aerodynamics.

In 1809, to demonstrate the effectiveness of his theories, Cayley constructed a full-size glider that flew successfully in ballast and then, for a few yards, even carried a boy. Thirty-four years later, following an idea put forward by Robert Taylor, one of his associates, Cayley produced an ingenious design for a 'convertiplane' – a boat, fitted with wheels, that had a superstructure supporting four large circular discs. The discs – arranged in pairs set at dihedral angles, to give the machine lateral stability – were intended to act as helicopter rotors. When they had raised the machine vertically to the required height, Cayley meant them to close and form circular wings. At the rear of the machine, he had provided a pair of pusher airscrews which were intended, then, to provide horizontal propulsion. The 'convertiplane' never got beyond the preliminary, try-out model stage.

By this time, Cayley was ageing, but younger men were carrying out, under the influence of his ideas, some historic experiments. Two of these men – W. S. Henson and John Stringfellow – produced, in 1842, a design for an 'Aerial Steam Carriage'. In the following year, after the two inventors had been granted a patent,

22 A museum model of the hydrogen balloon in which the first human ascent was made from Paris in 1783 by the physicist, J. A. C. Charles, with a mechanic

23 A museum production of Sir George Cayley's first model glider, 1804

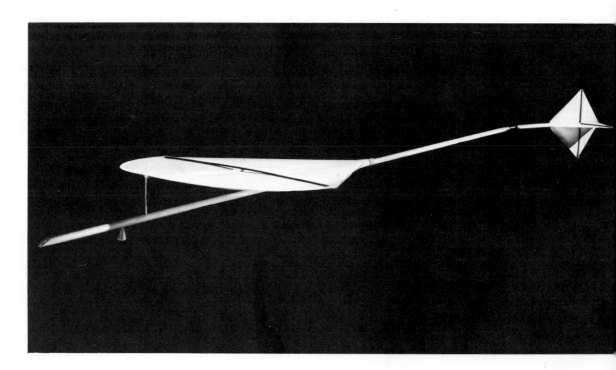

they published their designs, and these caused an international sensation, prints and sketches and even decorative handkerchiefs showing their 'carriage' being produced and sold all over the world. The two men intended their vehicle to fly regularly between London and India, providing the first properly organized air transport system in the world. Their ambitions were not realized, however, since the model they constructed to prove the effectiveness of their theories failed, in 1847, to pass its tests. Thoroughly cast down by this disappointment, Henson married and emigrated to America. His collaborator, made of sterner stuff, continued to experiment.

Stringfellow did not, at first, receive any proper reward for his single-minded devotion to the advancement of science. He had made a splendid little steam engine for the model of the Aerial Steam Carriage. Left alone, he fitted this engine into a more advanced monoplane model of his own design. He tried out this model, which had a wing span of 10 feet, in a large room in a disused lace factory, launching it from a wire runner and catching it, at the end of its all-too-short career, in a canvas sheet. By this brief journey, Stringfellow's monoplane became the first engine-driven model in the world to fly successfully.

Unfortunately for the triumphant researcher, no one of any consequence appears to have recognized the significance of his achievement, and having lost money by his activities Stringfellow gave up all attempts to rival the birds until the Royal Aeronautical

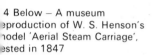

4 Below – A museum reproduction of W. S. Henson's model 'Aerial Steam Carriage', tested in 1847

5 Bottom – A museum reproduction of John Stringfellow's monoplane model of 1848

Society was formed in Britain eighteen years later. Being, then, encouraged to proceed with his investigations, he built a model triplane that weighed just under 12 pounds and had a wing area of about 28 square feet. The engine, which drove two pusher propellors, is believed to have produced about $\frac{1}{3}$ h.p. Stringfellow showed the model at the Society's first exhibition in the Crystal Palace at Sydenham, in South London, in 1868. It aroused a great deal of interest, one of the most inquisitive spectators being Edward, the Prince of Wales, later King Edward VII. For His Highness' pleasure and amusement Stringfellow made the model run along its launching and tethering wire, but it did not become truly airborne and it is usually written off as a failure. Like the equally land-bound Aerial Steam Carriage, however, Stringfellow's triplane exerted a powerful influence on later and more successful pioneers. The biplane, which remained the most popular type of European flying machine for nearly a quarter of a century, was foreshadowed directly by the designs of Henson and Stringfellow.

The first model aircraft to be driven by twisted rubber bands was made in 1874 by Alphonse Pénaud, who was a member of the French Aeronautical Society. Pénaud's model rose to a height of fifty feet or more, and then flew horizontally. Pénaud also intended to make a large man-carrying machine, but he fell sick and died at an early age before he had had a chance to achieve lasting fame. (He has not been entirely forgotten by model-makers, however. Charles Magrath, an American who, in the late 1920s, wrote several books about model aircraft, made a true-to-scale half size replica of Pénaud's masterpiece. Mounted on a polished pedestal, with an engraved name plate, this historic small model was presented by Magrath, shortly after World War 2, to the publisher of the *American Aircraft Modeler* magazine.)

26 Above left – A beautiful museum reproduction of Stringfellow's model triplane, 186

27 Above – A sketch of the rubber-powered model made by Alphonse Pénaud

28 Right – The Aeronautical Society's Exhibition at the Crystal Palace, London, in 1868

The German engineer Otto Lilienthal, who also tried to design large man-carrying aircraft in the last decades of the nineteenth century, is remembered with honour, too, by model-makers with a taste for aeronautical history, because his 'hang gliders' – which were really bat-like contraptions in which Lilienthal would hang from the framework by his arms, using his legs as an undercarriage – actually did fly. (From an artificial hill he had had built near Berlin, he managed to glide for nearly a quarter of a mile.) Tragically, Lilienthal was killed in August 1896 while he was using one of his standard monoplanes.

In the same year, on the other side of the Atlantic Ocean, Professor Samuel Pierpont Langley, the secretary of the Smithsonian Institution in Washington, D.C., and a scientist with an international reputation, came within a hair's breadth of being the first person to achieve the goal of lifting a human being into the air in any form of mechanical flight. S. P. Langley's story is one of the most moving, and ironic, in the whole long chronicle of aeronautical research.

It is entirely relevant to this book because Langley experimented for several years with small models of various configurations to which he gave the attractive but confusing name of 'aerodromes'. When one of these steam-driven models of Langley's made a circular flight of three-quarters of a mile, he decided that the time was ripe for him to build and fly a full-sized machine.

Langley's assistant in this enterprise was the skilled engineer C. M. Manly. After studying an ingenious rotary engine built by S. M. Balzer, Manly had managed to produce a remarkably light gasoline engine of the radial type – the first internal combustion engine designed specially for use in an aircraft – and this was installed in a large replica of the successful Langley model. Manly, himself, was installed as its pilot. Two attempts were made to launch the machine from Langley's house boat on the Potomac River below Washington, but on both occasions the launching catapult failed to clear the struts on the airframe, and the plane, arrested each time before it had become properly airborne, crashed into the river. Luckily, Manly was not hurt on either occasion, but after the second fiasco the authorities who had been financing Langley's experiments refused to provide any more funds, and the project had to be dropped. Langley was then made, by the national press, a figure of fun.

Nine days, exactly, after Langley's machine failed for the second time to become airborne, the brothers Orville and Wilbur Wright made the world's first powered, controlled and sustained flights at the Kill Devil Hills near Kitty Hawk. The Wrights would probably never have achieved this historic feat if they had not been prepared to study the problems of flight-control in greater detail

29 Right – A museum model of a 'hang glider' of Otto Lilienthal, 1895

30 Right below – A museum model of S. P. Langley's 'aerodrome' of 1903

than had the unfortunate Professor Langley. To acquire the necessary knowledge, the brothers had made a wind tunnel in which they had tried out numerous model wings and control surfaces. When they reckoned that they understood all the implications of their experiments – and not before – they made and flew a number of gliders. When, with these, they reckoned that they had solved the basic problems of flight, they constructed their first powered biplane. Innumerable models have since been made of this simple but effective machine. One of the finest – made by Christy Magrath in the late 1920s – is so realistic that even the flesh tones of the face of the 'pilot' lying on the wing are accurately reproduced.

The Wrights called their powered machines (appropriately) 'Flyers'. It was the third Wright Flyer, launched in 1905, that is honoured now as the first really practical airplane of all time as it could bank, turn and circle. And, it could fly for more than thirty minutes before it was compelled to land.

Ever since 1783, when the brothers Joseph and Étienne Montgolfier – paper-makers of Annonay, near Lyon, in France – sent a balloon with a cock, a duck and a sheep into the air before an

admiring crowd, the idea of making aerial voyages beneath great globes that were little more than 'bags enclosing clouds' had appealed to adventurous men. During the nineteenth century, ballooning became a fashionable activity for those who could afford it. Scientists, sportsmen and entertainers rose progressively higher and higher into the air under their inflated containers, and travelled further and further, until, by 1900, it seemed to many people as though the free lighter-than-the-atmosphere balloon would solve the world's transport problems cheaply, safely, and without the necessity for any of the new-fangled mechanical nonsense.

So, while Langley and the Wright brothers, in far-off America were wasting their time (the balloonists thought) experimenting with their heavier-than-air machines, innumerable air-minded fathers and uncles in Britain and other parts of north-west Europe were making 'miniature balloons' for the benefit of their admiring sons and daughters and nephews and nieces. Usually, each of these playthings – they were little more – would depend, for its 'lift', on a candle or a small spirit lamp fixed beneath a suitable aperture in the balloon's under surface. The fabrics from which these balloons were made were frequently inflammable, and a high proportion of the flights ended with a spectacular blaze.

It may have been this state of balloon-minded-ness prevailing in the Old World that caused a strange torpor to descend on those, in Europe, who might have been expected to be working busily towards the conquest of the air by powered flight. More than a year elapsed after the news of the Wright's triumphant success crossed the Atlantic before any mechanically-propelled flights were made on the weary old continent and, at first, these journeys were little more than tentative hops. (When the Brazilian, Alberto Santos-Dumont, on 12 November 1906, managed to make his biplane, that looked rather like a child's box kite, stay in the air for $21\frac{1}{5}$ seconds, his comparatively minor achievement was greeted with frantic applause from the bystanders.) Short as it was, that trip inspired many other Europeans to attempt to do better. Soon, Gertrude Bacon was to record her impressions of the first flight she made with Roger Sommer:

'The ground was very rough and hard, and as we tore along, at an increasing pace that was very soon greater than any motor I had yet been in, I expected to be jerked and jolted. But the motion was wonderfully smooth – smoother yet – and then – ! Suddenly there had come into it a new, indescribable quality – a lift – a lightness – a life! Very many there are now who know that feeling: that glorious, gliding sense that the sea-bird has known this million years, and which man so long and so vainly envied it,

31 A museum model of Santos-Dumont's unconventional flying machine called the '14-*bis*'. The maker gave it this name because he at one time tested it hanging beneath his airship 'No. 14'.

and which, even now, familiarity can never rob of its charm . . . You wonderful aerial record breakers of today and of the years to come, whose exploits I may only marvel at and envy, I have experienced something that can never be yours and can never be taken away from me – the rapture, the glory and the glamour of "the very beginning".'

An outstanding figure among these early seekers for 'the rapture, the glory and the glamour' was Alliott Verdon Roe, who, later, was to head the great firm of A. V. Roe (Avro), Manchester, England, that manufactured the *Anson* and *Lancaster* bombers and other exceptionally successful aircraft. A short account by Roe of the start of his career was published in the first issue of the *Amateur Aviator* in April 1912. His reminiscences, which showed how he increased the size of his models, in easy stages, until they became full-size airplanes, are of absorbing interest, today, to students of aeronautical history:

'... My first serious model was made on the lines of an Albatross, whose graceful antics I had admired so much when at sea as an engineer.

From my point of view this model was not a success (at least not so successful as I could have wished). I therefore tried another on the same lines as that of the Wright Brothers, of whom I had just at that time heard. I quickly found out that it was advisable to have a large plane in front or behind and from that time constructed my models with such, and good results were obtained with either type.

Gliders I made by the score, and very soon I found myself loaded with basketfuls of them.

About this time the *Daily Mail* offered £250 in three prizes for models making certain flights, so I immediately set to work and made a three-foot model, which I had flying within ten days of the competition.

As there was plenty of time to spare, I made some others eight

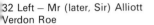

32 Left – Mr (later, Sir) Alliott Verdon Roe

33 Left below – A. V. Roe's 'Langley', seen at an exhibition at the Agricultural Hall, London, in 1907

34 Below – Another model at the 1907 Agricultural Hall exhibition

feet long by eight feet wide, and it was ultimately with one of these I won the *Daily Mail* Prize in April 1907, just five years ago this month.

Thus encouraged, I set to work on a full-size machine fitted with a 24 h.p. Antoinette engine, and in June 1908 managed to obtain a few short hops with it at Brooklands (airfield and race track).

Previous to this in the latter part of 1907, I ought to add, I obtained many flights in a machine towed behind a car. I used to regulate the height up and down by the front elevator. On one occasion the machine broke away from the car, and I was powerless to prevent the smash that followed. (They generally ended that way, and many exciting adventures befell me.) I remember vividly my boot heel was torn away as I was dragged among the wreckage. The tower's instructions were to let go as soon as the machine swerved away from behind the car, being attached to about 60 feet of cable; but I had the greatest difficulty in getting new hands to do this.

Unfortunately, the then manager of the Brooklands track was not at all sympathetic towards aeroplanes or aviation, in fact, instead of receiving encouragement, reasonable requests were refused and every obstacle placed in my way.

It was only on condition I would lend my shed on Race Days that I was allowed to stop at all, and just as I was reaching the hopping stage I was requested to remove my goods.

The shed was purchased by the authorities for a mere fraction of its cost.

After this I returned to London and started on designs and plans for a triplane with the engine forward, very much like our last triplane in general appearance.

After building the machine I rented some railway arches on Lea Marshes. Here many amusing and unpleasant experiences befell me.

Although the engine was only a 9 h.p. J.A.P. heavy motorcycle type, I managed to get many short flights rising to twenty feet in height.

Early one quiet morning I was just about to start some trials when the ground inspector of the Lea Marshes turned up and ordered me off the ground.

I therefore went to the next ground which I had used previously, but had not been there long before a gentleman in blue, plainly labelled policeman, bobbed up and took my name and address. Just at that time, however, Blériot flew the Channel and this made all the difference in the Inspector's attitude, for he too became interested, so all was easy and plain sailing again, and I was allowed to continue . . . '

Radio-controlled model of the Shinn 2150 posed in front of the prototype

Overleaf, a museum model of Sir George Cayley's 'convertiplane'

As flying passed out of the purely experimental stages, information became more generally available to model-makers through the medium of the press. In the early days of flying in Britain – for instance – the magazines *Aero* and, later, *Flight* provided short sections intended specially for aeromodellers. By 1913, a little more space for articles on model aeronautics was being allotted regularly in such magazines as *Model Engineer* and *Practical Mechanics*. *Model Aircraft* and *Model Aeroplane Constructor* were the first British periodicals to cater especially for devotees of the new hobby but they were quickly overtaken by the *Aeromodeller* which, managed with great efficiency by the legendary D. A. Russell, was largely responsible for the universal growth of interest in the subject.

Today, models of airplanes of historic vintages are made and collected with great enthusiasm in many different parts of the world. Organizations such as the Society of Antique Modelers in America and the Antique Model Aeroplane Society in Britain exist to keep modellers with these special interests in touch with one another and to make generally available to their members all the relevant information about ancient aircraft, and ancient models, that can possibly be collected. The approximately forty members of the British society believe that they have, between them, just about every plan, magazine or model publication ever produced in the English language prior to 1950!

A detail of a museum model of Henri Giffard's airship, which first flew in 1852, showing the single-cylinder steam engine

3 The Design and Construction of Model Aircraft

Model aircraft can be roughly divided into two principal categories – those intended to resemble, to a greater or lesser degree, some full-sized prototype, and the others that are created to act as miniature flying machines in their own right. Frequently, models of the latter kind look as though their designers have never even seen any conventional aircraft.

Clearly, the problems of design and construction that face the model-maker will vary according to the primary function of the finished work. In this chapter, matters of common interest to the makers – and admirers – of models of both types will be briefly dealt with. Some aspects of particular interest to 'scale' enthusiasts will be covered in greater detail in Chapter 4.

Most of the great pioneering figures who constructed their own working model aircraft in the earliest days of the hobby based their designs on the shape of the letter A. The main members of a typical A-fronted pusher monoplane entered for competitions between the years 1912 and 1920 would probably be made of birch wood, and they would be cross-braced with thin wire. The wings would be made of spruce sheet, with steamed ribs. In occasional models, they would have a frame of piano wire and would be covered, in these cases, with oiled silk. The twin airscrews would be made from wood steamed and bent to shape, or carved from a solid block of wood, or – again, occasionally – made by bending sheet aluminium. Each airscrew would be powered by a long rubber motor, and the pair would revolve in contrary directions, so that the unwanted effects of torque would be neutralized. (Torque is the force generated by a revolving propeller that tends to rotate a model in the opposite direction to that in which the propeller is turning.) Most of these early A-framed models were hand-launched, but wheeled undercarriages were occasionally fitted, and a few Rise-off-Ground (ROG) flights were recorded, evoking great excitement.

Not so generally popular, at first, as these A-framed models were the relatively simple 'stick models' developed at roughly the same time. Each stick model would be made with just one pusher or

35 and 36 The constructed skeletons of two model aircraft showing the careful work necessary before the outer covering is added

tractor propeller mounted on a single rigid-spar fuselage (spruce was particularly favoured for these strictly functional model aircraft bodies). By 1925, this rudimentary type of model plane had become the most commonly seen and flown in all civilized parts of the world. Go-ahead modellers then developed some little aircraft which had hollow-spar fuselages made from thin birch veneer. The outer surfaces of these fuselages were polished, and the models' rubber motors were usually fitted to them by external mountings. A firm of model manufacturers, A. E. Jones Ltd., won transitory renown by marketing models which had hollow veneer spar fuselages, inside which the strands of rubber of the motors ran freely in French chalk.

As soon as prototype aircraft were being produced commercially on a considerable scale in a number of countries, aeromodellers who studied them closely became dissatisfied with the unreality of their stick models. They did not find models made with 'profile fuselages' much more satisfying (a profile fuselage is cut from a flat sheet in such a way that the outline represents that of an actual full-sized aircraft, when seen from the side).

If it is to resemble convincingly the fuselage of a real aircraft, irrespective of the angle from which it is seen, they found that the model's fuselage has to be a little less rudimentary than either a single spar or a cut-out shape. A hollow tube of some kind could be converted for the purpose, they discovered. Such a tube may be very effective when used for a rubber-powered endurance model. More popular, though, with aeromodellers has been the simple, box-shaped fuselage that has, over virtually the whole of its length an upper surface, a lower surface, and two sides.

37 Right – A comparatively recent reproduction of an early twin-pusher rubber-powered model

38 The main members of a rudimentary box-type fuselage

Making a box-shaped fuselage of this kind is not a difficult proposition, even for the beginner. At its simplest, the fuselage can consist of four pieces of some thin sheet material (wood is generally used). These are cut out, and bent slightly, and joined along the edges – with some reinforcement – so that they finish as a smoothly streamlined form.

There is, today, a more popular and more satisfactory method of making a box-like fuselage. The principal components in a fuselage of this type are four strong longerons, or fore-and-aft members. These are braced and supported by lighter, but rigid, cross-pieces, and over the whole frame, a suitable skin is applied. A properly constructed fuselage of this kind will be both light and strong.

No matter whether it is to be rudimentary or complicated, any model aircraft that is intended to fly has to fulfil certain inescapable stability requirements. So, before building starts, a carefully considered design has to be produced.

Normally, the designer of a plane – whether it is a full-sized

39 Overleaf – Typical plans from which an aeromodeller may get the necessary information

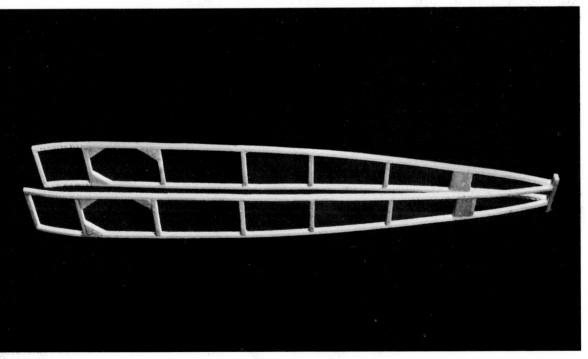

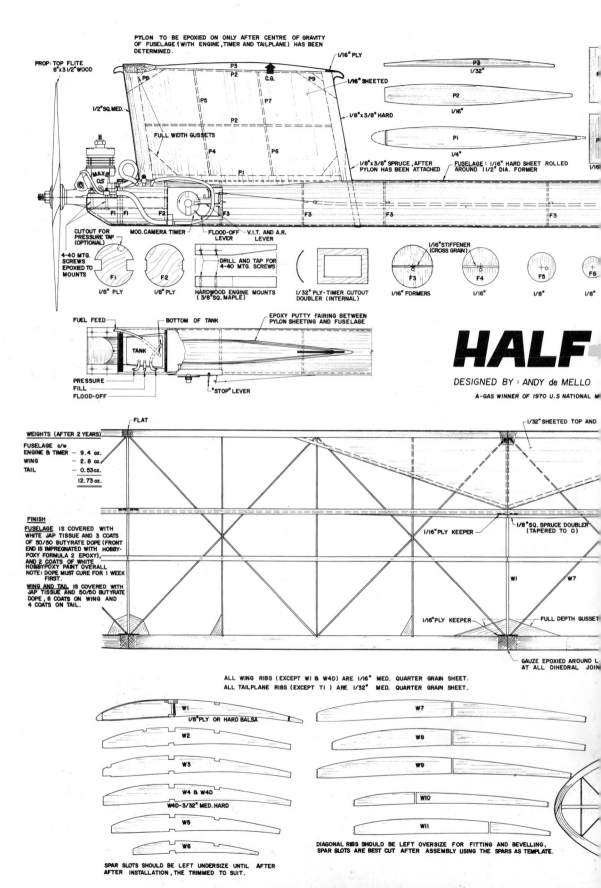

PYLON TO BE EPOXIED ON ONLY AFTER CENTRE OF GRAVITY
OF FUSELAGE (WITH ENGINE, TIMER AND TAILPLANE) HAS BEEN
DETERMINED.

PROP: TOP FLITE
8"x3 1/2"WOOD

1/2"SQ.MED.

MAX. QS

CUTOUT FOR
PRESSURE TAP
(OPTIONAL)

4-40 MTG.
SCREWS
EPOXIED TO
MOUNTS

MOD. CAMERA TIMER

FLOOD-OFF
LEVER

V.I.T. AND A.R.
LEVER

FULL WIDTH GUSSETS

1/16" PLY

1/16" SHEETED

1/8"x3/8" HARD

1/8"x3/8" SPRUCE , AFTER
PYLON HAS BEEN ATTACHED

FUSELAGE : 1/16" HARD SHEET ROLLED
AROUND 11/2" DIA. FORMER

P3
1/32"

P2
1/16"

P1
1/4"

F1   F2

1/8" PLY   1/8" PLY

DRILL AND TAP FOR
4-40 MTG. SCREWS

HARDWOOD ENGINE MOUNTS
(3/8"SQ. MAPLE)

1/32" PLY-TIMER CUTOUT
DOUBLER (INTERNAL)

1/16"STIFFENER
(CROSS GRAIN)

F3
1/16" FORMERS

F4
1/16"

F5
1/8"

F6
1/8"

FUEL FEED

BOTTOM OF TANK

EPOXY PUTTY FAIRING BETWEEN
PYLON SHEETING AND FUSELAGE

TANK

PRESSURE
FILL
FLOOD-OFF

"STOP" LEVER

HALF

DESIGNED BY : ANDY de MELLO

A-GAS WINNER OF 1970 U.S NATIONAL M

FLAT

1/32" SHEETED TOP AND

WEIGHTS (AFTER 2 YEARS)

FUSELAGE c/w
ENGINE & TIMER — 9.4 oz.
WING   — 2.8 oz.
TAIL   — 0.53oz.
                12.73 oz.

FINISH

FUSELAGE IS COVERED WITH
WHITE JAP TISSUE AND 3 COATS
OF 50/50 BUTYRATE DOPE (FRONT
END IS IMPREGNATED WITH HOBBY-
POXY FORMULA 2 EPOXY),
AND 2 COATS OF WHITE
HOBBYPOXY PAINT OVERALL
NOTE: DOPE MUST CURE FOR I WEEK
FIRST.
WING AND TAIL IS COVERED WITH
JAP TISSUE AND 50/50 BUTYRATE
DOPE, 6 COATS ON WING AND
4 COATS ON TAIL.

1/16"PLY KEEPER

1/8"SQ. SPRUCE DOUBLER
(TAPERED TO 0)

W1   W7

1/16"PLY KEEPER

FULL DEPTH GUSSET

GAUZE EPOXIED AROUND L
AT ALL DIHEDRAL JOIN

ALL WING RIBS (EXCEPT WI & W4D) ARE 1/16" MED. QUARTER GRAIN SHEET.
ALL TAILPLANE RIBS (EXCEPT TI) ARE 1/32" MED. QUARTER GRAIN SHEET.

W1
1/8"PLY OR HARD BALSA

W2

W3

W4 & W4D
W4D-3/32" MED. HARD

W5

W6

W7

W8

W9

W10

W11

DIAGONAL RIBS SHOULD BE LEFT OVERSIZE FOR FITTING AND BEVELLING,
SPAR SLOTS ARE BEST CUT AFTER ASSEMBLY USING THE SPARS AS TEMPLATE.

SPAR SLOTS SHOULD BE LEFT UNDERSIZE UNTIL AFTER
AFTER INSTALLATION , THE TRIMMED TO SUIT.

Full-size plans may be obtained from the N

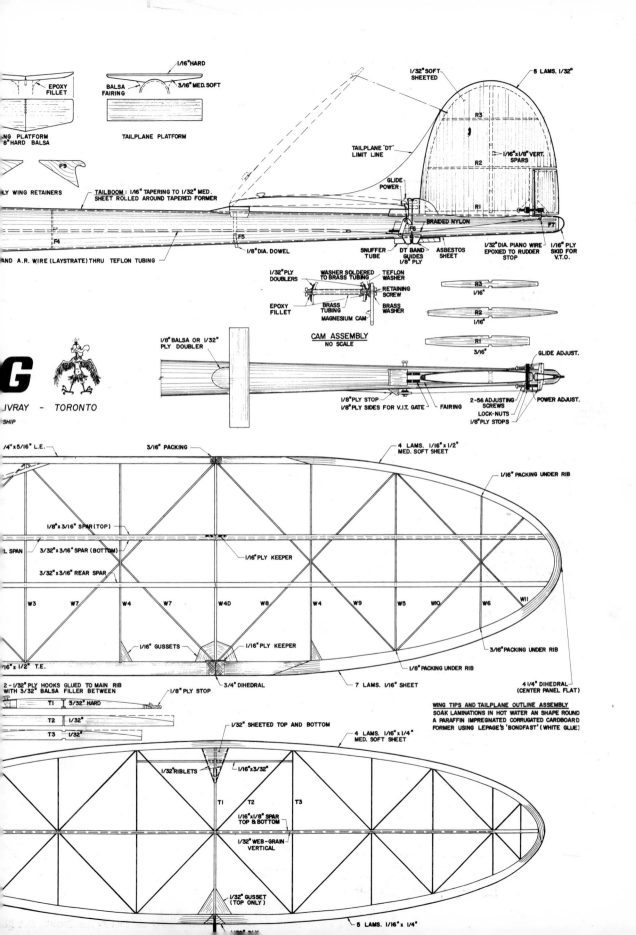

EPOXY FILLET

1/16" HARD
3/16" MED. SOFT
BALSA FAIRING

TAILPLANE PLATFORM

NG PLATFORM
8" HARD BALSA

P9

LY WING RETAINERS

1/32" SOFT SHEETED

5 LAMS. 1/32"

R3

TAILPLANE "DT" LIMIT LINE

R2

1/16" x 1/8" VERT. SPARS

GLIDE POWER

R1

TAILBOOM : 1/16" TAPERING TO 1/32" MED. SHEET ROLLED AROUND TAPERED FORMER

BRAIDED NYLON

F5

F4

1/8" DIA. DOWEL

AND A.R. WIRE (LAYSTRATE) THRU TEFLON TUBING

SNUFFER TUBE

DT BAND GUIDES 1/8" PLY

ASBESTOS SHEET

1/32" DIA. PIANO WIRE EPOXIED TO RUDDER STOP

1/16" PLY SKID FOR V.T.O.

F6

F7

1/32" PLY DOUBLERS

WASHER SOLDERED TO BRASS TUBING

TEFLON WASHER

RETAINING SCREW

R3
1/16"

EPOXY FILLET

BRASS TUBING

MAGNESIUM CAM

BRASS WASHER

R2
1/16"

CAM ASSEMBLY
NO SCALE

R1
3/16"

1/8" BALSA OR 1/32" PLY DOUBLER

GLIDE ADJUST.

G

IVRAY - TORONTO

SHIP

1/8" PLY STOP
1/8" PLY SIDES FOR V.I.T. GATE

FAIRING

2-56 ADJUSTING SCREWS
LOCK-NUTS
1/8" PLY STOPS

POWER ADJUST.

/4" x 5/16" L.E.

3/16" PACKING

4 LAMS. 1/16" x 1/2" MED. SOFT SHEET

1/16" PACKING UNDER RIB

1/8" x 3/16" SPAR (TOP)

L SPAN

3/32" x 3/16" SPAR (BOTTOM)

1/16" PLY KEEPER

3/32" x 3/16" REAR SPAR

W3   W7   W4   W7   W4D   W8   W4   W9   W5   W10   W6   W11

1/16" GUSSETS

1/16" PLY KEEPER

3/16" PACKING UNDER RIB

16" x 1/2" T.E.

1/8" PACKING UNDER RIB

2 -1/32" PLY HOOKS GLUED TO MAIN RIB WITH 3/32" BALSA FILLER BETWEEN

3/4" DIHEDRAL

7 LAMS. 1/16" SHEET

4 1/4" DIHEDRAL (CENTER PANEL FLAT)

1/8" PLY STOP

T1   3/32" HARD
T2   1/32"
T3   1/32"

WING TIPS AND TAILPLANE OUTLINE ASSEMBLY
SOAK LAMINATIONS IN HOT WATER AN SHAPE ROUND A PARAFFIN IMPREGNATED CORRUGATED CARDBOARD FORMER USING LEPAGE'S 'BONDFAST' (WHITE GLUE)

1/32" SHEETED TOP AND BOTTOM

4 LAMS. 1/16" x 1/4" MED. SOFT SHEET

1/32" RIBLETS

1/16" x 3/32"

T1   T2   T3

1/16" x 1/8" SPAR TOP & BOTTOM

1/32" WEB-GRAIN VERTICAL

1/32" GUSSET (TOP ONLY)

5 LAMS. 1/16" x 1/4"

aircraft or a working model – has to bear in mind three principal 'control axes' – the imaginary lines about which the aircraft has the ability to rotate.

The first of these axes is a vertical line that passes through the invisible, but immensely important, centre of gravity of the aircraft. (Picture this axis, if you like, as a string by which the aircraft can be suspended so that it can turn, as it moves forward, to left or right.) By using a vertical tail surface, the movement of the aircraft about this vertical axis can be controlled.

The second of the axes is a line that runs through the aircraft from nose to tail and passes, also, through the plane's centre of gravity. (This axis can be pictured as a horizontal spit on which the aircraft can rotate very much as a chicken can be turned while it is being cooked on a nose-to-tail skewer.) Known, often, as the 'lateral axis', this is the line about which the aircraft should be able to roll, as it moves forward, according to the movements of the correct control surfaces.

The third of the axes is the imaginary line that joins the wing tips of an aircraft, passing through the plane's centre of gravity. As the aircraft climbs or dives, it appears (if seen directly from the side) to rotate about this line exactly as a cut-out silhouette of the plane might rotate round a pin stuck through it at the fulcrum, or point of balance. When the nose of the plane turns upwards, the tail turns downwards, and vice versa. A plane that is not properly

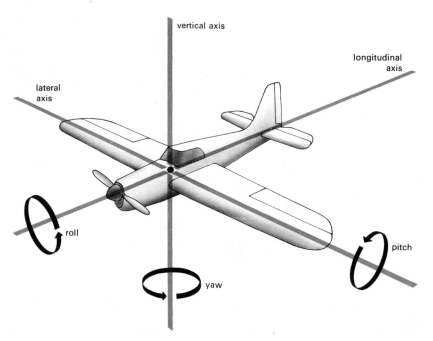

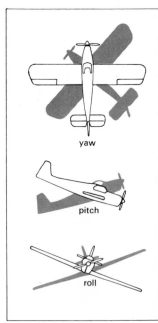

balanced about these axes is unlikely to fly far without coming to grief.

The design from which a successful working model aircraft can be made may be a new one altogether – possibly, a project conceived and drawn out by the model-maker himself, if he is sufficiently knowledgeable and inventive – or it may be a proved design obtained from some other source. Most commercially produced kits contain working drawings and, usually, detailed instructions for the assembly of the various parts. Plans are published, too, in all the magazines and journals that cater for aeromodellers. And, there are firms in many different parts of the world that help to satisfy the demand for reliable drafts.

Not much equipment is needed by the aeromodeller who decides to make his own working drawings. A flat surface, large sheets of paper, a ruler, and pencils are virtually indispensable. A T-square or triangular set-square is almost essential, too, though if it is necessary to improvise one can use any flat sheet material that has one corner accurately squared.

Clearly, it is not always possible for a design to be prepared to the same scale as the proposed model – a drawing printed on the small page of a magazine, for instance, may be intended to help with the construction of a fuselage or wing ten or more times as large. The important thing is to know the precise scale to which the plan has been drawn. If the plan is not drawn to full-size, then the

Left – The three principal control axes of a model aircraft

Right – Some important parts of a model airplane: 1 wing; propeller; 3 engine; 4 trailing edge; 5 canopy; 6 fuselage; stabilizer; 8 fin; 9 rudder; 10 elevator; 11 spinner; 12 landing gear; 13 flaps; 14 leading edge; 5 aileron

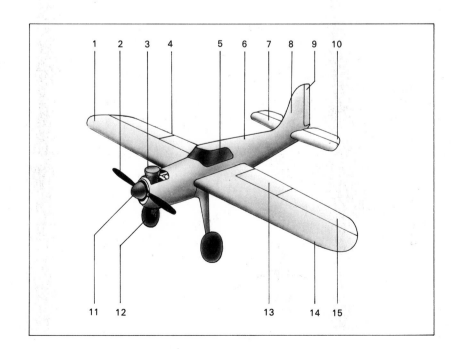

scale may be given as, for example, 1:24 or, more usually in the form:

$$\tfrac{1}{2} \text{ inch (of drawing)} = 1 \text{ foot (of model)}$$

If a model is to be made to larger dimensions than those shown on the working drawing, a draftsman's rule will be needed – on this, a number of different scales are marked. Alternatively, a network of small squares can be drawn on the plan and a similar network (only, with the lines further apart) can be drawn on another sheet of paper or on the material from which the model is to be made. Then, by reference to the smaller network, the points of intersection of the required outlines can be plotted on the larger network. Curves can be sketched-in lightly with a free movement of the hand or they can be drawn with a draftsman's French curve or with a 'spline' (a thin length of wood - frequently, balsa – that can be bent so that it passes through a number of previously determined points).

When a design for a model has been drawn out full size, it is usually necessary for the outlines of the various parts to be abstracted from the drawing of the general assembly. Most easily, they are traced-off on thin, translucent tissue paper that is made specially for the purpose. After that, the pieces of tissues are fixed to the wood from which the parts are to be made, clear 'dope' (a transparent adhesive usually made of some nitrate, butyrate, or cellulose substance) being normally used for the purpose. Alternatively, the wood can be placed under the full-sized design and the outlines of the various parts can be transferred using carbon paper. It is important, when either method is used, to have the grain of the wood running in the direction suggested on the plan.

The simplest kind of wing that can be fitted to a model aircraft is one that has been cut from a flat sheet of some thin, rigid material. If the wing of a model is left flat, though, it cannot be as efficient at providing 'lift' as a wing that has camber or airfoil shape. In certain instances, however – as, for example, where a model has to react instantly to radio control, or where a control-line model has to obey the slightest movement of the operator's hand – the neutral quality of a flat wing or a wing with a symmetrical section may be a positive advantage. A model fitted with wings with a pronounced camber, flown under either of these forms of control, is liable to 'fight' the signals transmitted to it by the pilot on the ground.

Dihedral – the upturning of a wing surface which, Sir George Cayley discovered, helps to preserve the stability of an aircraft – can be provided for a flat-sheet wing of an elementary kind if the material is scored, or cut partly through, along the nose-to-tail centre line. If the two sides of the wing are then bent upwards to the required angle, their 'set' can be preserved by the application of a

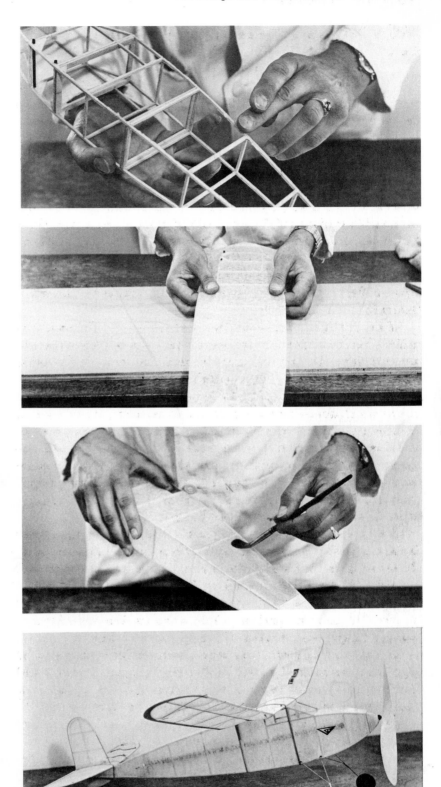

42 Covering a box-type fuselage with tissue (from top to bottom): spreading the paste with a finger; pulling the tissue out to remove wrinkles; doping; the completed job

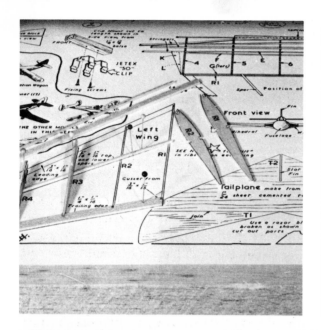

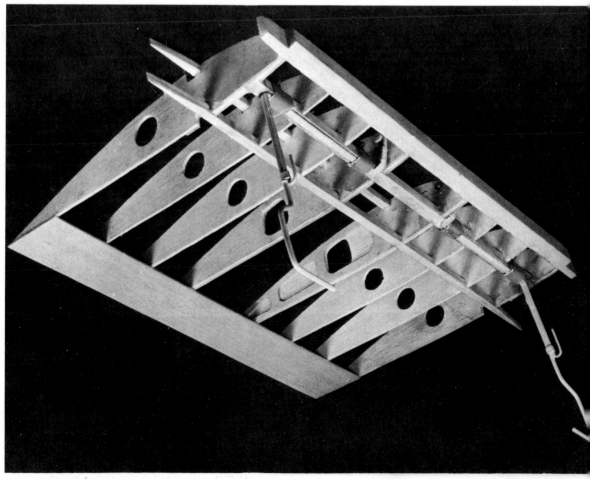

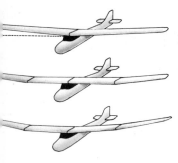

3 Left – The components of a wing being assembled on the plan (left); pins hold the components in place until the cement sets (right)

4 The centre section of the wing of a model aircraft under construction. The main members of the landing gear may be seen in position.

5 Above – Three types of dihedral, top to bottom: straight dihedral; tip dihedral; polyhedral. The arrow indicates the dihedral angle.

few coats of aeromodellers' cement – supplemented, perhaps, by a strip of silk or some similar material that has been impregnated with this quick-drying adhesive liquid.

A wing fabricated from a number of components will depend for its strength on a well-designed and carefully constructed frame. At its simplest – as, for example, in a wing intended for a beginner's rubber-powered model – this frame may be merely a rectangle, made from lengths of stripwood cemented together, and given some extra rigidity by the addition of one or more straight cross-pieces.

In a slightly more complex wing – intended, perhaps, for a small, free-flight model to be powered by a miniature internal combustion engine – the principal load-carrying member may be a single strong spar, set more or less at right angles to the nose-to-tail centre line of the model. Joining this spar to the carefully shaped pieces that form the front or 'leading' edge and the rear or 'trailing' edge there will be a number of ribs, each of which will correspond in profile to the cross-section profile of the wing at that particular distance from the model's centre line. Single-spar wings have one serious drawback – they are liable to warp. Distortions of a wing's principal aerodynamic surfaces can have disastrous effects on a model's performance. To obviate this, stronger structures are usually provided for models whose wings are to have a wider span than (say) 36 inches.

One of these 'jumbo' wings may well have two or more spars. These may be set above each other, where the wing section is thickest, or, alternatively, they may be spaced out at approximately equal distances along the chord of the wing. The leading and trailing edges will probably be made from pieces of wood. The former, which may have to bear the brunt of many accidents and collisions, will be a really strong member. It will be trimmed and sanded until its outline becomes a perfectly smooth continuation of the contour of the model's rib. The trailing edge, lovingly tapered until it ends in an edge almost as sharp as that of a knife, will do as little as possible to impede the air flow. Thin sheet wood will probably be used for the ribs and for any strengthening webs that may be fastened between the spars. It may also be used for the upper and lower coverings. If it is, the whole wing will be almost as strong as a similar wing made of aluminium.

Few ideas, in the whole history of aircraft design, can truly be said to be wholly original, but the development, shortly before the end of World War 2, of the delta wing can only be described as revolutionary. Created by the German, Professor Alexander Lippisch, just as aerodynamic experts in several countries were foreseeing the difficulties that would have to be overcome when aircraft, with increasing speeds, attempted to pass the daunting

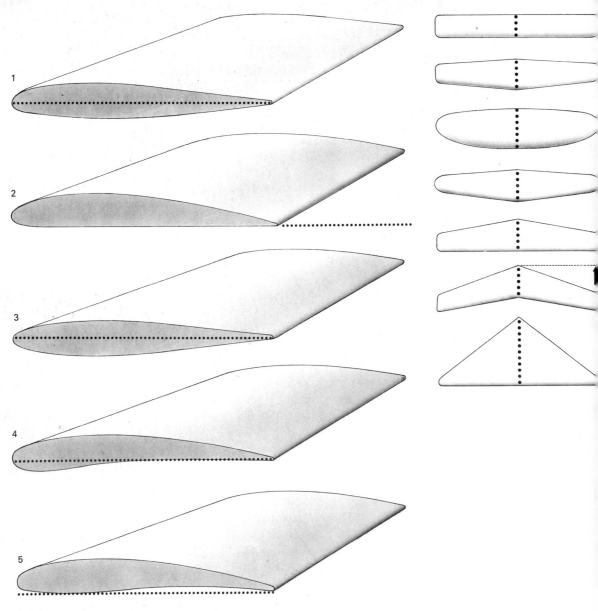

'faster-than-sound' barrier, the triangular wing, which had its front or leading edges swept sharply back, and a straight back or trailing edge, solved several baffling structural problems before they had really to be seriously grappled with. The Allied teams, studying captured German material after the end of hostilities found Lippisch's DM-1 delta-winged glider which, before Adolf Hitler's war effort was overcome, had been intended to serve as the prototype for a coal-fuelled fighter. The glider, completed and carefully shipped over the Atlantic, was exhibited at the United States Air Force Museum at Dayton, Ohio, without ever having effectively left the ground. Its influence on the history of aircraft

46 Left – Airfoils: (1) NACA 23012 – widely used on full-sized aircraft, not suitable for models; (2) Clark Y – most suitable for free-flight models; (3) NACA 0012 – for control-line and radio-control aerobatic; (4) Grant X-9 – for biplane models; (5) RAF 32 – rubber driven model

47 Above – Wing shapes found in model aircraft, from top to bottom: rectangular tapered; elliptical; two combination types; swept back (the arrow indicates sweep-back angle); delta

48 Carving the nose block of a
model aircraft after it has been
fitted to the airframe

was enormous, however. Today, replicas of delta-winged aircraft,
such as the Douglas *Skyhawk*, which has been a first-line fighter,
fighter-bomber and ground support machine for more than fifteen
years, play a big part in the international aeromodelling scene.

Lift, in a forward-moving model aircraft, is usually created by
two separate but complementary factors – the 'angle of attack', or
tilting up of the leading edge of the wing by as much as 6 degrees;
and the shape of the airfoil as seen in a number of sections. In a
fairly typical and one of the most universally admired airfoil
sections – the 'Clark Y' – the wing has a curved upper surface and
a flat under surface. Most of the lift created by a wing of this kind

is due to the difference of air pressures created above and below the wing as the aircraft moves forward. Having further to travel than the air that passes beneath the wing, the air that passes over the curved upper surface has to accelerate, forming a partial vacuum.

New Zealand has produced one of the greatest experts on the scores of different airfoil sections favoured by the world's most successful model-makers. It took John Malkin, of Upper Hutt, several years of research to go through every modelling magazine, book and newsletter in his own collection and those of his friends, classifying and plotting all the information as he acquired it. Now, his book is on sale in many different countries and is recommended as the authoritative guide.

As energetic in his researches as John Malkin, has been the eminent American aeromodeller and expert on airfoil geometry, Donald R. Monson. In 1963, while he was hunting, Monson managed to acquire the wings of a Red-tailed Hawk, and he wrote an erudite article about them for the *Minneapolis Modeler*. With the article, Monson published an outline drawing of one of the bird's wings. On this, he had superimposed the airfoil sections taken at three spanwise locations. To help anyone who might wish to make a pair of hawk-like wings for a model aircraft, he added a table of dimensions, calculated to three places of decimals. 'The wings stayed limber for about a week', Monson recorded reassuringly, 'and all measurements were made before drying out of the wing spoiled the original airfoil shape.'

The wings of some model aircraft (like the wings of many prototype planes) are fitted with ailerons – or, as they are often called, 'flaps'. These are movable sections positioned at the trailing edges of the wings. They are hinged about axes parallel to the lengths of the wings. Lowering an aileron increases the angle of incidence and therefore the 'lift' of that portion of the wing. Raising the aileron has exactly the opposite effect. By 'trimming' or adjusting the ailerons, an operator is able to control any rocking of the plane, about its longitudinal axis, that may develope.

Not all the wings fitted to model aircraft are directly attached to a fuselage. In 1938, Carl Goldberg, the lively proprietor of the great model firm of Chicago, Illinois, produced a design in which the wing was raised high above the fuselage on a fin-type mount now generally known as a 'pylon'. Goldberg's model proved unusually stable, exceptionally reliable when under power, and almost free from the ill-effects of torque. (In a pylon model, this unwanted force is counterbalanced by the pressure that the slipstream is able to exert on the side of the pylon, on the underside of the wing, and on any fin that may be fitted at the rear.) The configuration that Goldberg has devized with his characteristic ingenuity has been

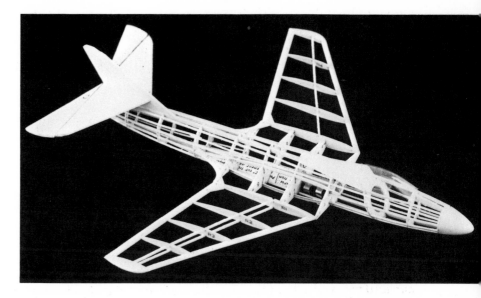

49 The airframe of a model Hawker *Hunter* with nose block and stabilizer in position

favoured, since, for an enormous number of medium-sized models.

A wing, by itself, is usually too unstable to fly without the assistance of a 'stabilizer'. In most model aircraft, as in most full-sized prototypes, this will take the form of a horizontal tail plane that exerts the pressure necessary to keep the wing at the required angle and will bring it back to that angle after the plane has dived or if it 'stalls' or suddenly starts to lose lift. Associated with the stabilizer, which will usually be constructed in a similar way to the wing, is the rudder or vertical tail that has the job of holding the model on a steady course and helps to turn it to left or right as the operator requires.

Balsa – from a tree grown principally in South America – is the lightest and most easily worked of all the woods available to the amateur craftsman. It can be cut with a sharp knife or razor blade almost as easily as can cheese. Pieces of it can be joined quickly and permanently if some blobs of specially prepared 'cement' (a solution of cellulose acetate) are placed between the surfaces to be united. The chief disadvantage of balsa – its lack of strength – can be partially overcome if its outer surfaces are covered with a smooth, thin material such as silk, which will provide some reinforcement.

The uses of balsa for flying models were fully exploited for the first time in the United States during the years immediately following World War 1. By 1930, the American enthusiasts who had been experimenting successfully with the new and tractable material were ready to storm the conservative citadels of Europe. In that year, an American modeller captured, for the first time, the celebrated Wakefield Cup (see p. 76). The model that triumphed over all the Old World opposition was a light, all-balsa machine.

The day of the contest was windy and unpleasant, and almost everyone present thought that the American model, which seemed so flimsy, would stand no chance against the sturdier, more orthodox entrants. After the event, British modellers changed their views, and the following year saw some radical changes in European model plane building techniques.

Balsa comes in a number of different densities. For parts that have to take a considerable load (such as the longerons that are usually the main fore-and-aft members of a model aircraft's fuselage) balsa of a fairly heavy density should clearly be chosen. Parts that are not subjected to much stress or strain, such as the subsidiary ribs of a wing, should be made from lighter balsa, so that the aggregate weight of the model can be kept down without weakening it in any way.

Most suppliers try to indicate the density of their woods by marking each piece with a figure that represents the probable weight of a cubic foot. (This may range from 6 pounds, approximately, at the lighter end of the scale, to 16 pounds or more at the heavier end.) A few suppliers use their own at-a-glance colour codes to grade their wares, but these codes vary according to the

50 A balsa airframe showing one method of fabricating a stabilizer

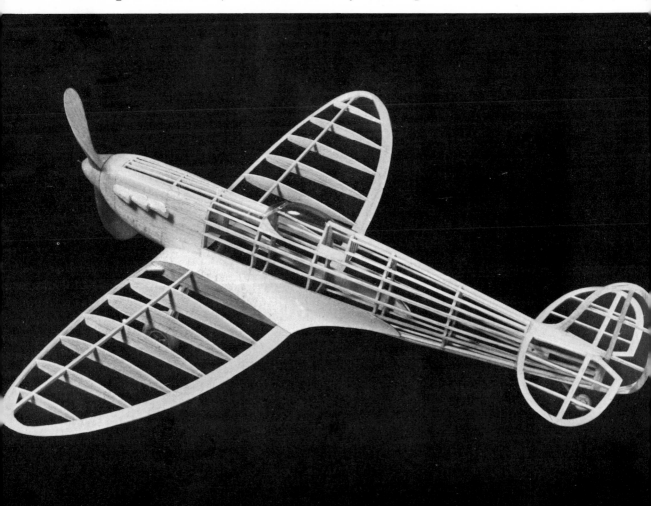

individuals who have devised them, and are liable to be confusing. The experienced aeromodeller generally becomes quite clever at selecting balsa. He – or she – will weigh each sheet in the hand and will assess it, quite accurately enough for all ordinary purposes, as as 'light', 'medium', or 'heavy'.

Having made the framework of a fuselage, a wing, or a stabilizer unit, the model-maker has next to choose a covering material suitable for the size and shape of the model. On a very small light plane only a very thin fabric or film can be used. On a larger model, a heavier and stronger skin will usually be necessary as it will have to stand up to more severe punishment.

Paper has been used for covering many hundreds of thousands of model planes. It can be obtained in almost as many different grades as there are types of aircraft, the thinnest and lightest – known, usually, as 'Japanese tissue' – being often chosen for the midget, rubber-powered models with which many beginners obtain their first taste of the thrills of the air. Thicker papers, such as those made from bamboo, are used for covering models where thousandths of an ounce, or a gram, do not have to be taken into careful consideration.

51 Covering part of a fuselage with sheet balsa

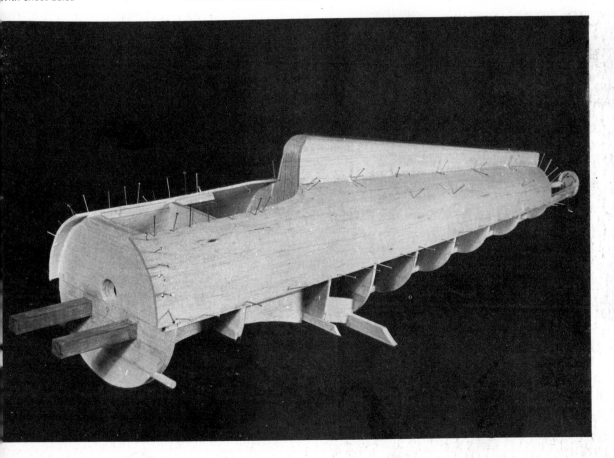

Some specially prepared papers known as 'wet-or-dry' can be used, as their name suggests, in the state in which they come from the manufacturer, or they can be soaked with water and then drained of surplus moisture. These are coverings that will adapt themselves easily to the subtlest of curves and will present, when they have dried out, a surface that is entirely free from wrinkles.

Silk is a strong covering, and in an untreated state it is conveniently light. Unfortunately, it happens to be porous, so, to be effective, it has usually to be sealed with the liquid known to aeromodellers as 'dope' (see p. 54). The doping treatment can add significantly to the weight of the silk and, in consequence, to the weight of the model, and because the dope, as it dries, can cause the silk to contract, it can set up serious stresses – enough, sometimes, to warp disastrously the frames over which the silk is stretched. Nylon is used by many modellers today instead of silk, but as it does not shrink as noticeably as silk does when it dries, it has a greater tendency to form wrinkles. Materials in which silk and nylon are combined are recommended by some manufacturers as being the most satisfactory of all.

One of the thinnest materials now used for covering model airplanes is called 'microfilm'. This cannot be bought in sheets, ready-made – it has to be prepared by the model-maker. To make it, one needs an extensive water surface (such as that provided by an ordinary household bath) and a spoonful or two of the special fluid which can be bought from almost any store that caters for aeromodellers. When this liquid is dropped on the water it spreads out almost instantaneously and becomes a film of uniform thickness. Immediately after that, the film solidifies to become a clear flexible sheet. This sheet can be raised from the water's surface on a suitably shaped wire frame.

One of the most successful rubber-powered model aircraft ever made – it has established several world records, has been World Champion once (when the Championships were held in Romania), runner-up once (in Rome) and has dominated European indoor flying almost since its appearance – is the brain child of the talented Czech modeller Jiří Kalina. Kalina covered the two halves of his wings in separate operations, using a film made according to this formula:

2% Eucalyptus Oil
15% Amylacetate
83% Nitrocellulose
5 drops castor oil for a 200 gram batch.

To make this film adhere to a balsa framework, Kalina recommends the use of beer, though he does not specify what sort!

62 The tissue covering of a wing
shrunk with a water spray after
assembly

If an accurate census were taken of all the millions of operational model aircraft in the world today, it would certainly be found that those driven forward by one or more propellers would drastically outnumber the gliders and the models propelled by rocket or jet-type engines. So, the enormous number of propellers that have to be produced to equip these models will be readily appreciated.

The action of a model aircraft propeller can be likened, for convenience, to that of a corkscrew – as the corkscrew is turned, radially, it tends to move forward into the cork. So as a model's propeller is turned radially, it will move forward into the air before it. As far as possible, the modeller tries to avoid the loss of 'thrust' (or forward propulsive force) through slippage.

For every model, there is one kind of propeller that will produce better results than any other, and an expert will try to find, in each case, the most suitable combination of these factors:

The diameter of the propeller (measured from tip to tip)
The pitch of the propeller (that is, the distance the propeller will move forward in theory, during each complete revolution), and
The area of the blade or blades of the propeller.

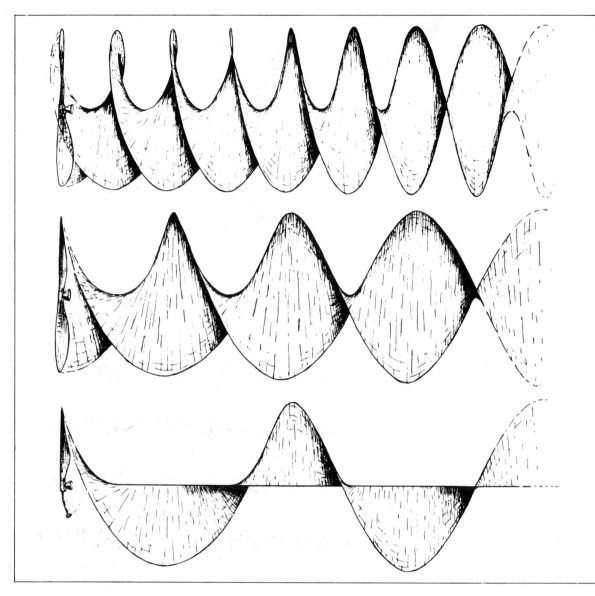

With most gas (petrol) engines, the maker will recommend that only propellers of certain outside diameters should be used. Free-flight modellers who wish their planes to climb almost vertically find the low-pitched propellers give the most satisfactory results. High-speed models used for control-line contests, on the other hand, are invariably fitted with high-pitched propellers.

Not many aeromodellers today bother to carve propellers to their own specifications from blocks of wood, since there are so many excellent commercially-produced wooden propellers on the market. It is not unusual, though, to see an expert make some slight adjustments to one of these in order to make it extra-efficient.

53 Part of Bob Meuser's drawing, based on sketches furnished by Hewitt Phillips, which illustrates the path traced by the blades, top to bottom, of a low-pitch, two-blade propeller; a high-pitch, two-blade propeller; and a high-pitch, one-blade propeller

Factory-made nylon propellers are preferred to wooden propellers by many modellers. Though these may not produce quite
as much 'thrust' as wooden airscrews, they are less liable to snap
and they are, therefore, often reckoned to be more suitable for use
where landings are likely to be rough.

Propellers for models intended for indoor flying – a very popular
branch of the hobby at the present time – have to be (literally) as
light as feathers, since flight endurance under these conditions is
liable to be reduced by every thousandth of an ounce of additional
weight. Some indoor-model propellers, then, are carved from the
softest and lightest balsa so that their blades are almost as thin as
paper. Others are most delicately fabricated, with outside edges

and supporting ribs made from extremely thin strips of balsa, the whole being then covered with microfilm. At the sixth Indoor World Championships held in the vast R 101 Airship Shed at Cardington, Bedfordshire, England, in August 1972, Merrick (Peter) Andrews of Bogota, New Jersey, the first man known to have broken the magic 30-minute 'barrier' in indoor flying, won the official title against contenders from fourteen different countries with two 'best' flights totalling 71 minutes 9 seconds. Andrews' winning model, including its propeller, weighed a mere 0·038 ounce.

On some types of model aircraft – particularly rubber-powered planes intended for endurance flights – single-blade propellers, though less sightly than conventional symmetrical airscrews, have been found to be unusually effective. In every case, a small heavy

counterweight has to be used (in place of the 'missing' blade) to produce the necessary balance.

All aeromodellers whose aircraft are intended to fly have to ensure somehow that their models will have as many happy touch-downs as possible, and no more disastrous crash landings than can be avoided. Where the stresses to be absorbed on landing are likely to be extreme – as, for example, in high-speed control-line models – a plane's undercarriage has to be abnormally sturdy (or it is likely to be crushed or snapped off at the roots at the moment of impact) and flexible, rather than rigid, so that it will resume its normal shape as quickly as possible after all danger of fracture is past.

A free-flight model may need only one wheel, or possibly two, mounted on a light wire strut, or struts, and supplemented by some downward-turned skids attached to the rear stabilizer. The landing gear struts of scale models may have to be streamlined to resemble those on the prototypes. Undercarriages that can be raised or lowered at the operator's wish are often fitted, today, to radio-controlled planes by sophisticated designers.

During the time that has passed since the earliest working model aircraft were first launched, several new materials suitable for the construction of miniature planes have become available to the amateur craftsman. Polystyrene, sheet plastic and glass fibre are three only of the synthetic substances that are favoured now by many modellers for special purposes, and more may well have come on the market by the time this book appears. Aeromodelling, like commercial engineering generally, has had to keep abreast of the times.

Occasionally, this has meant that new and entirely unexpected problems have had to be dealt with, by the official bodies that control aeromodelling.

Extra-sophisticated adhesives, for instance, have produced some bad publicity for a hobby that should be almost entirely innocuous. (The discovery, by a journalist, that alpha-cyanoacrolate rapid bonding adhesives carry warnings that contact with the skin is dangerous has led to the publication of some lurid stories of stuck-together fingers being cut apart in hospitals.) While these adhesives may well call for some extra care when in use, they are unlikely to be chosen by any but very advanced and discerning modellers.

5 A single-blade model aircraft propeller in position

6 Commercially produced landing gear for model aircraft

4 Rubber-powered Model Aircraft

Ever since Alphonse Pénaud made the first elastic-driven model aircraft in 1874, twisted strands of rubber have been used by innumerable aeromodellers to provide a cheap, clean and safe source of power for their miniature flying machines. Until very recently there have been few enthusiasts who have not learned the elementary principles of model aviation from some neat and lively little rubber-powered craft with a wing span limited to 12 inches or even less, and a single straight member, usually made from wood, that has acted as a rudimentary fuselage. Many of these comparatively crude but educationally priceless models have been made from kits. Comparable kits are still being sold in large numbers by several successful companies.

The development of the rubber-powered model airplane in Europe and America was stimulated excitingly by the public flights made by the Wright brothers – near Le Mans, in France, at the US army acceptance trials at Fort Meyer, Virginia, and elsewhere in the United States – after they had succeeded in finalizing satisfactory agreements with the French and American Governments.

One of the earliest innovators in this field was Percy Pierce, who eventually became vice-president of the Aero Club of Pennsylvania. At the edge of twelve, in 1906, Pierce built his first model airplane. Two years later, he exhibited a rubber-powered model at the first aerial show held at Morris Park, New York, under the auspices of the Aeronautical Society. This model was a biplane, six feet long, made of dowel stick covered with cambric linen. Next year, Pierce built and flew a model that is believed to have been the first ever to be constructed, anywhere, of the classic 'pusher' type. There is no doubt that this model has had the best performance of any made up to that time.

By 1911, the first associations of aeromodellers were being formed in several countries. In America, for instance, Willis C. Brown, with a few of his friends, founded the grandly named 'Independent Aero Club' (what it was independent of, nobody knew, because it was the only club of its kind within the knowledge of its charter members). Brown's first model – a replica of the monoplane in

7 John Gard, veteran rubber-power model flyer and several times a member of the U.S. World Championship teams, launches his Wakefield Model straight up. In about five seconds, after the initial burst of power from the tightly-wound motor, the model will relax into a more leisurely climb.

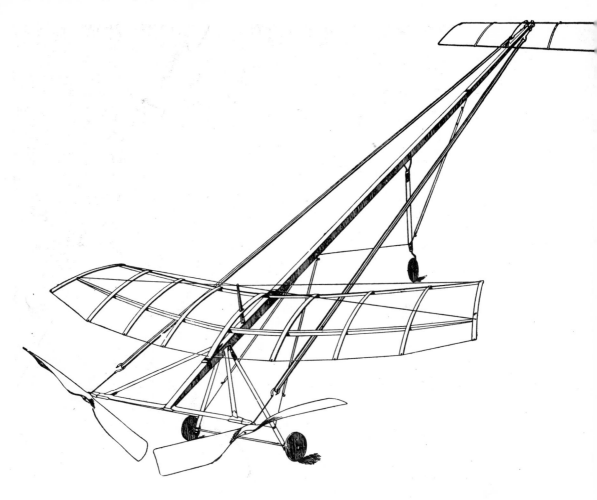

which Louis Blériot made the first flight across the English
Channel early on Sunday morning, 25 July 1909 – had a framework of chestnut strips glued together and wound with thread.
The framework was then covered with silk from an old umbrella.
The plane, powered with several rubber strands knotted together,
'presented a formidable appearance', recorded a contemporary
writer, 'but was particularly outstanding in its lack of good flying
qualities.' In spite of this initial reverse, Brown went on to become
the first President of the American Academy of Model Aeronautics
and has been called by many 'The Father of Model Aviation'.
Brown's energy was proverbial, earning him in the AMA's Official
History this unconventional accolade:

> 'Dynamite when aroused. Floored spectator at IGMAA [Inter-
> national Gas Model Airplane Association] meeting when latter
> chased and threatened a contestant. We forget the count . . .'

Competitive flying between the operators of rubber-powered

58 A sketch of the historic rubber
powered machine that won the
first Wakefield Cup contest

A simple rubber-powered
model designed by Paul McIlrath
and marketed in the Classic kit
series of the American Sig Mfg Co.

Overleaf above – a rubber-
powered scale model of a Fokker
III monoplane. It was flown
triumphantly by Bryan Webster in
the 1972 American National
Championships.

Overleaf below – Christian
Schwartzbach, a Danish expert,
with his Wakefield model that was
selected as one of the American
National Free Flight Society's
Models of the Year in 1972

models started in Europe and America before World War 1, and
was resumed in earnest shortly after hostilities ceased. International
rivalry was stimulated in 1927, when a Mr F. de P. Green, a
prominent member of the SMAE in Britain, approached Sir Charles
Wakefield, a wealthy industrialist who had done a lot to improve
the design of the internal combustion engine by sponsoring the
production of record-breaking airplanes, racing cars and speed
boats, and asked for his support. Sir Charles agreed cheerfully to
extend his considerable influence into the model aircraft world,
and promptly presented a very handsome cup and prize money
sufficient for three years for an open-to-all-comers competition
for rubber-powered models.

The first 'Wakefield Cup' contest was won by a Mr T. H. Newell,
with a plane that flew for 52·6 seconds. Two years later, a low-wing
hardwood machine owned by a Mr R. N. Bullock won the contest
with a flight that lasted 70·4 seconds. It was unusual, for that time,
in that the formers of the fuselage and the leading and trailing
edges of the wings were made from spring steel wire.

In 1930, for the first time, the Wakefield Cup was won by a competitor from America – Joe H. Ehrhardt of St. Louis, Missouri, whose little all-balsa model, mentioned in Chapter 3, had a 'best flight' of 155 seconds. Ehrhardt's plane was exceptionally light – it weighed only 2½ ounces – and its propeller revolved at about 450 r.p.m., as against the British average of 900 r.p.m. British modellers learned from this reverse the value of lengthening their motor runs by fitting larger propellers to their machines.

In the following year, the contest for the Wakefield Cup had to be held – according to the rules – in the holder's country. The outstanding duration machine in Britain in that year was a large low-wing all-balsa model designed and constructed by the Mr. Bullock who had won the cup in 1929. This airplane had impressive climbing power, looked very handsome when it was in the air, and (under the prevailing American influence) had an 18 inch diameter balsa propeller which revolved quite slowly. The model was sent to America, and flown by proxy. It clocked up a flight of 162 seconds, which was confirmed as the longest ROG airborne journey to be achieved, up to that date, by any British model aircraft. This flight, impressive as it was by existing European standards, only earned the machine a humble fourth place. The winner, again, was J. H. Ehrhardt.

Having suffered defeat in two successive years, the leading British modellers really began to stir themselves. They would have to send a properly organized team to America, they realized, if they were ever to retrieve the Wakefield Cup for their country. Without first-hand experience of flying conditions on the other side of the Atlantic, their quest would be hopeless. So, 'Wakefield Trials' were inaugurated in order that the best possible team might be selected to represent the Old World. The cost of transporting to America the chosen competitors, with their models, proved prohibitive until Sir Charles (by now, Lord) Wakefield put his hand into his very deep pocket and defrayed the greater part of their expenses.

In 1932, Gordon S. Light, of Lebanon, Pennsylvania thought he had taken the trophy from Ehrhardt, but Light's flight was disallowed, as the date of the contest had been postponed. Three years later, however, Light made aeromodelling history when he crated his model and sent it to England, to be flown by proxy by Thomas H. Ives of London. Ives beat all his own team mates with Light's model and as a result had to endure much good natured ribbing from his fellow nationals. His sportsmanship did a lot to promote transatlantic good feeling, however, and encouraged the promotion of more international events, to which adequately financed official teams could be sent by a growing number of countries.

62 Previous page, above left – A close-up view of the folding propeller assembly on Bob White's International Rubber-powered Class Wakefield model

63 above right – The American Academy of Model Aeronautics awarded a university scholarship in aeronautical engineering to Susan Weisenbach, seen here holding one of her successful rubber-powered models

64 Below – Bob White stretch-winds the rubber motor of his outstanding Coupe d'Hiver model

A close-up of a museum model of the Manly-Balzer petrol engine of 1902, installed in Langley's 'aerodrome'

Overleaf, a museum diorama of the first flight in 1903 of Wrights' Flyer

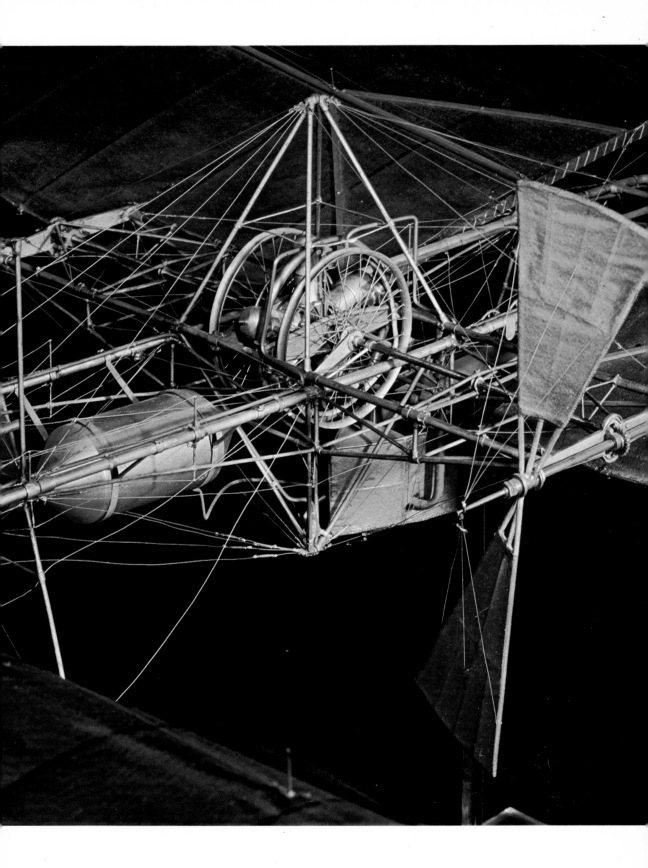

From the earliest days of the Wakefield Cup competitions until 1937, the winning model came every time from Britain or America. In that year, E. Fillon of France broke this dual monopoly by taking the trophy from Albert Judge, of Great Britain, with three flights that averaged 6 minutes 13 seconds. Twelve months later, James Cahill of Indianapolis, Indiana, took the trophy back to the United States with flights that had an average duration of 10 minutes 54 seconds.

Remarkable as this feat was, it was made to appear almost insignificant in the following year, when teams from the United States, Britain, Canada, France and South Africa, with a single entry from New Zealand, saw a phenomenal flight made by a plane entered by Dick Korda, of Cleveland, Ohio. Korda's home-designed model had an initial motor run of sixty seconds. This burst took it up to 200 feet, when the propeller folded back, as intended, and the model glided down half-way to earth. At this juncture, an entirely fortuitous 'thermal', or upward current of warm air, took over and the plane was carried up to a height of 1,500 feet or more, at which level it sailed in circles immediately over the judges for a seemingly endless period of time. When, at long last, it glided down to earth, the official verdict was that it had been airborne for 43 minutes 49 seconds. This, combined with two less spectacular flights, gave Korda an average of just under sixteen minutes – sufficient to keep the trophy in the United States by a comfortable margin.

As well as learning, quickly, how best to exploit the boosting effect of rising currents of relatively warm air, the cleverest American modellers of this period were responsible for one of the most important advances ever made in the operation of rubber-powered model aircraft when they conceived the idea of 'stretch-winding' their elastic. Today, this practice is almost universal, as it not only increases the probable duration of a flight, but it also lessens the chances of damaging the rubber.

Stretch-winding – the name is almost self-explanatory – requires the services of at least two people. While Number One operator holds the model, Number Two operator attaches a winder (usually, a brace that has a wire hook held in the chuck) to a suitable loop fitted to the propeller shaft. Number Two operator then walks away from the model so that the rubber is stretched to approximately five times its normal length. Turning, he starts to wind up the motor, gradually walking towards the stationary model as he winds, and as the skein of rubber strands consequently becomes shorter. Handled in this way, the rubber strands are allowed to bed into each other snugly, without their edges becoming frayed.

World War 2 put an effective damper on all international contests between rubber-powered model aircraft, as it did on so many other light-hearted human activities. Even on a relatively parochial

close-up of a model showing e engine installation in the 'rights' Flyer

scale, modellers in the combatant countries had problems because rubber became suddenly both scarce and expensive. Those who were lucky enough to have some pre-war stock took the greatest possible care of it, while less fortunate modellers were forced to resort to such measures as cutting up old automobile and bicycle inner tubes in order to be able to continue model flying.

Shortly after the end of hostilities, a committee was set up by the AMA in America to get things going again (Korda's cup having been held by the Academy during the war years). Among the important jobs the members of the committee were expected to do was the provision of proxies who could, and would, fly the models sent from foreign countries by people who were unable, for any reason, to cross their national boundaries. The committee had to remain almost inactive for nearly three years – until sufficient aircraft model-building material was available in all the relevant parts of the world. Then, in 1948, they held an excellent if slightly limited meeting – the first since before the Battle of Britain – at Akron, Ohio.

In 1949, the Wakefield Cup contest was properly reconstituted as part of an impressive International Model Week programme, scheduled to take place in the first part of August. The AMA managed to scrape together enough money to send a team from America to

65 Phil Klintworth studies air temperature as a guide to possibl thermal currents before releasing his fully wound rubber-powered model

the meet at Cranfield Aerodrome, in England, but, in blustery weather with gusty winds of up to 30 m.p.h. to make flying difficult, Aarne Ellila of Helsinki, Finland won the coveted trophy for his country for the first time. Ellila's model, prime among 92 competitors, managed to clock up an average of 183·3 seconds.

Throughout the post-war period, competitions for rubber-powered models have continued to cause a certain amount of excitement, though the conditions of many of the principal contests have had to be radically changed, to suit this more sophisticated age.

As late as 1940, for example, the airframes of 'Wakefield' models could be made more or less as the designers pleased, subject only to the need to get the planes to rise off the ground, and to remain airborne for longer than all their rivals. But the rubber motors in those good old days were not subject to any limits and, in consequence, too many modellers were achieving performances that would have amazed Lord Wakefield if he had been alive. So, the rules had to be altered, to make these superlative flights a little more difficult to achieve.

A start was made in the early 1950s, when the rubber allowance was restricted to 80 grams (about 2·75 ounces). This meant that each 'Wakefield' airframe had to weigh at least 5½ ounces if the total minimum weight of the model was to be brought up to the

56 Cameron Ackerly of Canada, having wound his Wakefield model, watches other models to see if they are going up in thermals or dropping in down drafts, before launching his own

required 230 grams (about 8·11 ounces.) Some confirmed rubber-powered plane operators regarded this, at first, as the death-blow dealt to their particular hobby. They soon discovered how to overcome the new limitation, however, and soon the rubber allowance had to be reduced to 50 grams (about 1·75 ounces). At this stage, the rule that all 'Wakefield' models had to rise off the ground under their own power was discreetly scrapped. Written off, too, were certain outdated regulations that dealt with fuselage cross-sections.

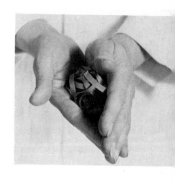

67 and 68 Multi-strand rubber motors need special care: lubrication (above); winding to form a taut even skein like a rope (right)

Then, the wind of change really began to blow. As soon as model owners realized that under the new dispensation they would no longer have to worry about the propellers of their planes fouling the ground on take-off, they started to experiment with propellers of very much larger diameters. (Some eye-catching 'Wakefield' models of this vintage were fitted with giant props that measured more than 2 feet from tip to tip.) These great blades provided extra efficiency, since they produced, during the nearly vertical climb from the initial launch, much the same effect as the rotors of a helicopter. Stalling – a complete loss of lift resulting from too steep an angle of attack, which had been the bugbear of the older 'Wakefield' models – was virtually eliminated.

Experiments were made, too, with models of many unorthodox designs. Scandinavian aeromodellers who remained faithful to rubber power produced some extraordinary prototypes which had thin airfoils, long and slender fuselages, and tiny stabilizers. These surprising and strictly functional machines – sent up to great heights by the initial thrust of their engines and sustained, thereafter, like gliders, by thermal currents – put up performances that were both spectacular and consistent.

In an attempt to make it a little easier to separate the men from the boys, the 'Wakefield' rubber allowance was reduced once again in 1966. This time, it was reduced to 40 grams. A motor as small as this has to be wound almost to breaking point if its full potential is to be realized. This makes its power output almost impossibly difficult to control. (There is one spectacular burst of energy and all is virtually over.) So, mini-craftsmen with a flair for gadgetry have had a glorious time since then, developing such devices as propellers that 'flare', or alter the pitch of their blades at the ground-pilot's behest, and time-operated cams that will change the trim of a model just as the initial power burst of the engine starts to taper away into a slow unwind.

However well-designed a rubber-powered model aircraft may be, it is not likely to give satisfactory results for long unless the rubber is looked after with the greatest care. Those who prepare such model planes for competitions tend to become especially fussy. Most of these rubber-motor experts have a favourite lubricant to

which they think all others are vastly inferior – their pet nostrum may be castor oil, or a combination of glycerine and soft soap thinned with water, or some other solution compounded according to a secret recipe. The most thorough operators wash their rubber motors after each series of flights, before they are put away into store. This removes the lubricant, of course, so that the rubber has to be treated again before it is brought back into use, but it also ensures that no small sharp particles of grit are left to cause any damage to the strands. Dried, carefully dusted with talcum powder, and coiled individually in screw-top jars, rubber motors given this treatment usually remain in the best possible condition for a number of events.

Most experts today use black Pirelli rubber (manufactured by the Italian motor-tyre company) believing that this only will conform to the high standards they demand. Even so, these exacting people recognize the fact that rubber is liable to vary appreciably from batch to batch, even if it comes from the identical factory. So, they test the Pirelli products they buy as carefully as a connoisseur of wines will examine, with his palate and the tip of his tongue, the offerings of his favourite vineyard.

9 A rubber-powered model
helicopter

A close-up view of the rotor-
de mountings of the model
copter shown on the previous
e

As recently, even, as 1971 the relative qualities of different kinds of rubber were being discussed seriously on an international level. At the first Scandinavian Wakefield Symposium held in Malmö, Sweden, in January of that year the allegedly disappointing quality of the current Pirelli rubber was discussed. Those modellers who had laid down a stock of Pirelli rubber of the 1962 vintage were very nicely placed, it was generally agreed, since that year produced the best Pirelli rubber ever. The Pirelli rubber sold to aeromodellers in 1971 was wider than usual – each strand was 7 millimetres (about 0·28 inches) across – but the delegates thought that it had a poor energy storage capability. Having thus cosily assessed the ruling Pirelli standards, the delegates turned to the problems of lubrication. No one had any very new ideas to offer. Some of the delegates used castor oil, still, while others preferred a mixture of soap and glycerine. Both groups declared their intention of sticking to their usual ways.

5 Model Flying Boats and Seaplanes

There are two types of aircraft that rise from, and return to, water surfaces rather than land, and they are known, usually, as 'flying boats' and 'seaplanes'. As models of such aircraft can be divided into the same categories, it will be necessary, first, to define the two terms.

A flying boat, as its name implies, has a single boat-like hull. This has to be carefully designed so that the plane will be as stable as possible when it is resting on, or taxiing over, the surface of the water. In some cases, sturdy projections known as 'sea-wings' or 'sponsons' may be added to the hull's sides, both to port and starboard, to lessen the risk of the plane tipping over in either direction. Often, small buoyant pontoons or 'floats' are fitted beneath and near the ends of a flying boat's wings so that if the aircraft does tilt seriously the effect of one of these 'tip floats' touching the water's surface will help to restore the machine's equilibrium.

The fuselage of a seaplane does not need to resemble the hull of a boat in such an obvious way, as it is kept off the water's surface by one, two or three of the aforementioned 'floats'. Although free-wheeling designers intent on performance rather than appearance sometimes make water-borne models that look like no real-life prototype ever seen, the usual conformation of a full-size seaplane calls for two fairly long and relatively narrow floats only – a matching pair, arranged so that they are parallel to, and a little distance from, each other – with, sometimes, a small extra float fitted to the underside of the tail.

From the earliest days of the commercial manufacture of aircraft, the problems of producing successful flying boats and seaplanes have stimulated some of the industry's most ingenious designers, and several distinguished prototypes have made aeronautical history. Models of flying boats and seaplanes have, correspondingly, attracted a great deal of interest and are still quite popular with the members of the societies which concentrate on 'old time' machines.

One of the first men to concern himself with full-sized seaplanes was the Englishman, Noel Pemberton-Billing. Pemberton-Billing

R.'O. Lehman's Twin Otter io-controlled scale model plane. This is one of the largest le models yet flown.

entered aviation in 1904, when he built a man-lifting glider, but he soon decided to devote his energies to constructing 'boats that will fly and not just aeroplanes with floats'. In October 1913 Pemberton-Billing took the name 'Supermarine' as his telegraphic address. In March of the following year he showed his first flying boat to the public. This machine – the P.B.1 – had a single tractor engine mounted between the wings above a cigar-shaped hull.

The outbreak of war, five months later, distracted Pemberton-Billing's attention, temporarily, from amphibian craft. In nine days' frenzied activity he designed and built a single-seater fighting airplane for the British Royal Flying Corps. This fighter, so hastily produced, has gone down in history as the direct ancestor of the Supermarine *Spitfire*, which, with its eight guns and its superb manoeuvrability, became one of the most vital weapons of World War 2.

In the years that followed the ending of hostilities in 1918, Pemberton-Billing's Supermarine Company went from strength to strength. In 1919, the company launched a commercial flying boat, the Channel Type, which found buyers all over the world. Three years later, the company compounded this success when the Supermarine *Sea Lion II*, a single-seat flying boat powered with a single 450 h.p. Napier Lion engine, won the International Schneider

2 Left – A museum model of the aunders-Roe *Princess*. The rototype was one of the largest ying boats ever constructed.

3 Left below – A plastic kit odel of the seaplane once used the Japanese Navy for bservation

4 A model of a seaplane of chneider Trophy vintage

75 A free-flight model of the Vickers-Supermarine *Seagull* flying boat

76 Above right – A testing tank at the works of Saunders-Roe Ltd, through which model seaplanes and flying boats could be towed

77 Even land-based aircraft may be compelled to land on water. Here is a model undergoing tests

Trophy race for Britain by travelling at the then astounding speed of 145·7 m.p.h.

And that was only the first of Supermarines' Schneider Trophy and world's speed record triumphs. Three years after, Supermarines' S4 seaplane, powered with a 700 h.p. Napier Lion engine, pushed the world's speed record up to 226·75 m.p.h. In 1927 the Schneider Trophy was won by the Supermarines' S5 seaplane, which raised the record, in the same year, to 283·67 m.p.h. In 1928, the same Supermarine seaplane travelled at 319·57 m.p.h. In the following years its successor, the S6, powered by a 900 h.p. Rolls-Royce engine and piloted by Squadron-Leader A. H. Orlebar, set up a new world's speed record of 357·7 m.p.h. In 1931, the Schneider Trophy was won outright by Flight Lieutenant John Boothman (later Air Marshall Sir John) in one of the last Supermarine seaplanes to earn international fame. Boothman's speed of 342·7 m.p.h. was surpassed, shortly after, by Flight Lieutenant G. H. Stainforth, who really punished the Supermarine S6B Seaplane, with its Rolls-Royce engine, to lift the world's record, for the first time ever, above the 400 m.p.h. mark. Aeronautical research at this period owed much to a Lady Houston, who, when the British Air Ministry failed to provide official financial assistance for the Schneider Trophy effort, dipped into her own pocket and made a last-minute contribution of £100,000 towards the expenses.

In the design and production of the early full-sized seaplanes and flying boats, many baffling problems had to be solved. As the cost of making even one prototype was liable to run into tens and even hundreds of thousands of pounds, and as there was always the possibility that some unforeseen hazard might result in the total loss of the craft being developed, some method had to be found by

which the designers' theories could be tested before their brain-children were given their final expensive form. Fortunately, the scale model – relatively cheap, even if of the highest quality workmanship – proved quite suitable for trying out new ideas. By submitting models to exhaustive tests, the innovators minimized the risk of some crippling disaster happening to their products at a later stage.

The chief difficulties encountered when moving models are used for such trials result from the lack of space available for control instruments and recording devices. At the National Physical Laboratories at Teddington, near London, and in the research departments of the principal aircraft manufacturers it was found advisable to construct long and deep tanks, well supplied with ancillary equipment which included mechanically operated wave-making machines.

Messrs Saunders-Roe Ltd, of East Cowes in the Isle of Wight, relied for a long time on two such tanks. The first – a towing tank – was spanned by a platform designed to run on rails set along its sides. This tank was used, principally, to investigate such characteristics as the longitudinal stability of a model in calm water and in waves, the model's resistance, and the effects on it of spray. When tests were being carried out in this tank, the model under examination would be coupled to the overhead platform which could achieve speeds up to 40 feet per second even when towing the model and carrying measuring equipment and as many as four observers.

The second tank at Saunders-Roe was used for free launch tests. In this kind of trial the model would be fired from a catapult at one end of the tank and would be in free flight before it came into contact with the surface of the water. This produced some very realistic effects and was used, additionally, for experimental work on the possible consequences of forced landings on water by land-based aircraft.

Eventually, Saunders-Roe found that some of the exact data they required could not be obtained from towed models or from solid models catapulted into indoor tanks. They needed to know – to quote only one example – more about the performance of a flying boat when it was taking off from a surface broken by very large waves. The flying boat would be accelerating, that was obvious, but its acceleration would not be constant because as it hit each wave the plane would tend to slow down. To investigate this erratic behaviour, the firm's designers decided to use models which could taxi under their own power.

The more complex self-propelled models they evolved were built, usually, of wood. Some of the models were powered by small compression ignition engines that drove propellers, but more often rocket engines were fitted, because of their greater reliability. The fuel used in the rockets was hydrogen peroxide. The motors were very robust – so much so that when, on one occasion, a model accidentally plunged into the water, the motor continued to propel the little 'flying boat' along quite happily below the surface.

While full-sized seaplanes and flying boats were attracting world-wide attention, and while their designers and pilots were extending so spectacularly the frontiers of human knowledge, amateur model-makers were attempting to win a more limited fame with their own small Rise-off-Water (ROW) craft.

Even before World War 1 had started, a lively correspondence had taken place in the British magazine *Flight*, which reserved certain of its columns exclusively for news of the model-making fraternity. In those days, seaplanes were called 'hydro-aeroplanes', and in an interesting discussion on his favourite subject a model-maker named G. P. Bragg Smith suggested that the floats fitted to model hydro-aeroplanes should be long and narrow – their length should be 12 to 15 times their breadth, he stated categorically. And, they should be provided with a step on the under-surface, he insisted, to help with the rise-off. This was a new idea at that time, and it did not go down well with everyone. V. E. J. Johnson, who edited the model news section of the aviation journal *Flight* at that time, did not agree, for a start. He advocated the use of wider floats, with a maximum length-to-width ratio of 9 to 1. 'Should a hydro-aeroplane have one float forward and two aft or vice versa?' another correspondent asked. The *Flight* readers' opinions on these matters were varied and were clearly based on uninformed guesswork.

By 1914, a world record for a ROW flight by a model flying machine had been established. The successful craft was a rubber-powered 'hydrobiplane' constructed and operated by F. Whitworth – a name that was soon to become famous in aeronautical circles. His model remained airborne for just 37 seconds.

After that, the progress made in this branch of model aeronautics was slow, rather than spectacular. In the international competition for model seaplanes held in 1930 (the prize was a cup presented by a Lady Shelley), not one model succeeded in rising from the water.

In the following year – the year in which British modellers learned from their American cousins the advantages of all-balsa construction – a high wing all-balsa model seaplane made by a young Englishman named Tony Willis managed to raise by a comfortably large margin the world's record for an ROW flight. Willis' success raised a storm of controversy. Conservative modellers claimed that his little seaplane, which was fitted with three tiny floats, was not properly seaworthy. One very articulate member of the council of the SMAE urged publicly that before

A commercially produced
model seaplane available in kit
form

future competitions for the Lady Shelley Trophy were held, the
models entered should be compelled to undergo some flotation
test, to see if they were capable of floating on the surface of the
water for more than a few seconds without being blown over or
without their floats becoming waterlogged. Before long, the preliminary trials suggested by this zealous legislator were made
mandatory by the rules, as we shall see.

In 1932, the Lady Shelley Cup was won by a Mr T. H. Newell,
whose model seaplane remained airborne for 46·7 seconds. Several
other competitors managed to heave their models up into the air for
shorter, but still inarguably successful flights. It was no longer such
a remarkable feat to get a model seaplane off the water's surface and
to keep it in the air as it had been in previous years. Before 1932's
bitter winter had settled down on the British Isles, an aeromodeller
named G. Merrifield from Bournemouth, on the south coast, had
put up a really fine official world's record of 90 seconds, with his
large three-float model seaplane.

The development of a petrol engine small enough to be used in
a model aircraft offered some new possibilities (and posed some
new problems) to the designers of miniature seaplanes. In 1943
one of the most energetic of these innovators – Lieutenant Colonel
C. E. Bowden – recorded his memories of his early attempts to set
up a world's record for this particular kind of model. Observing,
first, that the petrol-driven flying boat was an especially intriguing
type of power-driven craft because, to be successful, it had to be
both a stable airworthy machine and also a seaworthy machine
that was stable on the water, Lieutenant Colonel Bowden went on:

'. . . The strange-looking craft that I evolved in order to set up the first officially observed flight off water took off from Poole Water, about 1937, just above Hamworthy. A model petrol flying boat was a completely unknown quantity at that time, so there were no previous data to draw from and therefore the boat had certain exaggerated features to guard against the troubles I foresaw would have to be overcome to make a model stable both in the air and on the water. As a result, the boat had too large a wetted surface and was reluctant to get off the water with the 9 c.c. Brown engine originally fitted, but it was perfectly stable on the water. It would fly with perfect stability after a push start or hand launch on 9 c.c., and it would land and sit on the water in quite a severe wind and sea.

The problems I had to face were many. I was stationed at the time in the Midlands far from any suitable water and I had to get two official SMAE observers to come down for one day to some selected stretch of water, and it had to suit their convenience and my leave period. I had to ensure that my full-sized little speed boat was available on the selected water at the time decided upon; also the weather had to be suitable; so you will agree that in this busy world it was not easy to get all these factors to coincide!

I chose Poole Water for my leave, and trailed my little speed boat behind my car from the Midlands, hoping that the weather would suit, and the official timekeepers recognised by the SMAE would be able to make it on the date arranged. My leave was short and the days went by, my wife expected me to fit in other holiday pursuits besides flying model flying-boats, and

81 One of the earliest model seaplanes of which there is now any record — the Whitworth 'hydrobiplane'

the weather was bad! As a result of all this I only got in one or two flights and I had to assist the boat off the water because I found the engine power was just not quite enough. On one occasion it got off unassisted after a long run, because the water had just the correct "popple" to assist unsticking, also there was just enough breeze to help the take-off.

I knew that all these circumstances were most unlikely to repeat themselves on the day arranged for official observation! I therefore fitted an old "Atom" two-stroke 14 c.c. engine that I had by me; in fact the same engine with which I had put up one of the very early land 'plane records, which remained unbeaten for several years. This engine had a lot of power but was heavy according to the advanced standard of those flying-boat days, and it therefore upset all my balance arrangements of batteries, etc., on the 8 ft.-span boat, just to make things a little more unlikely!

Anyhow, in went the engine at the last moment, and I had no time to test the boat before the fateful day. The weather was fairly reasonable, the time-keepers arrived and my speed boat started! I dared not make a trial flight as I felt if things were not so good there would be no observed flight at all.

Those of you who have not done any water flying cannot appreciate what may happen to an overheated little petrol engine that dives into salt sea water. There is unlikely to be any more flying that day, and if there is elektron in the engine's construction, as there was in my 14·2 c.c. (*sic*) engine, the engine must be stripped at once or the corrosion due to salt water will seize everything solid.

Colonel Bowden's 6cc model
ing boat at rest in Gibraltar
rbour

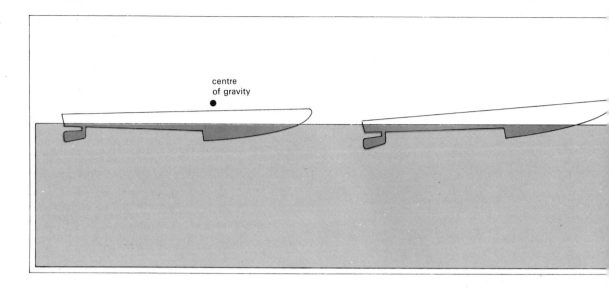

centre
of gravity

The compression of the 14·2 c.c. engine was fairly high as it had been hotted up for model hydroplane racing, after it had retired from landplane work. As a result of this high compression I had to use two flash-lamp batteries for flight.

In order to get an approximate balance I had to sling these batteries along the hull well aft, but this was guesswork without a test flight.

The boat got off well, but those infernal batteries were just too far back and the machine climbed at a pretty fierce angle and was stallish. This appeared to affect the flow of petrol. In those days I used gravity feed on this particular engine to a carburettor with midget float chamber. *Now* I should suck up the petrol!

Anyway the engine eventually cut out and the boat landed with rather a wet splash the right way up and had the decency to sit on the water for master to retrieve. But nothing would induce that engine to start again that day.

I therefore contented myself with having set up the first rise off water record for petrol flying-boats and determined that I would, at some later date, have another go at it with a better boat, incorporating the knowledge I had gained, *and* when I could get leave, weather, water and official timekeepers to synchronize. In the meantime I was ordered off to Gibraltar where official timekeepers just did not exist . . .'

Free-flying model seaplanes and flying-boats are not often matched against each other now in competitions, though the rules of the FAI do state that models of these kinds must rest on the water at take-off, must be held by the competitor in such a way that their natural position on the water is in no way modified, and

83 A diagram showing a model seaplane float in four positions during rise-off-water, from left to right: at rest; during take-off run; when only the step and aft parts are in contact with the water; clear of water resistance

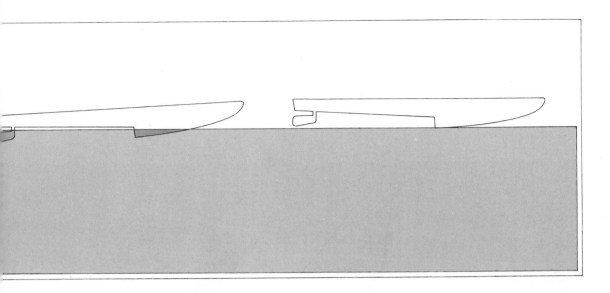

84 Right, above — A radio-controlled model seaplane made by William Aarts of the Netherlands. 85 Centre — Aart's model nearing rise-off-water speed. 86 Bottom — A twin-engined model seaplane with floats that are not wholly satisfactory. The centre of gravity is too far back, creating excess drag.

must be released without any assistance whatsoever on the part of the competitor. Prior to the take-off, a flotation test of one minute must be imposed on each model. During this time it must float on the water entirely on its own. (After winning first place in an indoor ROW event in Boston, Massachusetts, the late Ralph W. Brown disqualified himself, in a letter written to the contest director. In his excitement, Brown reported, he had forgotten to float his

7 Left — A floatplane version of
the German radio-controlled kit
model *Taxi*

8 Above — Water rudders on
model flying boats can be
radio-controlled. Here is a fine
model descending to the water
surface

model as called for by the rules. This piece of good sportsmanship
put Brown's stock up considerably with all his friends.)

The design of floats for model seaplanes and flying-boats is still
a matter of controversy, as it was in 1914, though most modellers
now agree that a float of any true-to-scale type must have a step
on the underside to help the float break free from the water surface
on rise-off. Research has shown that to be really effective, this step
should be positioned very slightly in front of the centre of gravity
of the model.

In some of the colder parts of the world, where the rigours of
winter tend to last for a frustratingly long time, keen modellers often
now fit skis on their planes so that they will rise from, and land on,
snow. Normally, a ski intended for use on a working model plane
will be made of some light but strong material such as plywood,
plastic or glass fibre, it will be reasonably short (to keep down its
weight) and relatively wide (to prevent it from sinking too deeply
into the surface of soft snow). Accidents may happen if the tips of
the skis fitted to a model plane meet the snow surface, on landing,
at too steep an angle so that they dig in. To prevent this, it is
customary to tilt the tips upwards by a few degrees. Sophisticated
model-makers use springs, pivots and other devices to ensure that
their skis operate with a reasonable margin of safety.

6 Scale Model Aircraft

Disinterested observers who attend aeromodellers' meetings for the first time are liable to point out that few, if any, of the aircraft on view look very much like 'the real thing'. There will probably be some good grounds for their complaints, as scale modelling, being an activity that demands very high standards of craftsmanship, only appeals to the enthusiast who is notably handy and extraordinarily patient. So, true-to-scale models that emulate real full-sized prototypes are not likely to be as numerous as the models that have been designed and constructed for the sake of their potential performance, but they are sure to attract attention and, if they have been faithfully carried out, may even fall into the 'minor works of art' category.

The urge to produce a true-to-scale replica of a particular aircraft often hits a modeller with such force that the problem of choosing a suitable prototype does not arise. One of the finest scale models ever seen – an award-winning replica of a Ford Trimotor monoplane – came in 1970 from the work bench of the American craftsman Fulton H. Hungerford. Hungerford had started to make models of Ford planes some thirty-six years earlier:

'... When I was in the fourth grade in school, Ben Gregory came to our town barnstorming with his Ford. I drew up the plans for the Ford then, and I still have that drawing. In my sophomore year in high school I was commissioned to build a rubber-powered flying scale model of the Ford for fifty cents. It flew and the customer was happy. Those were hard times – probably 1934 ...'

In 1969, Hungerford decided to make a scale model of a Ford and to enter it for the American National Championships. He admitted, later, that he had set himself an exceptionally difficult task:

'... Actually, the selection of a Ford Trimotor for an event which required high performance was not very wise. Everything about

A flying scale model of a kker triplane seen in flight

the Ford was a challenge: the covering, the drive units, and the stability. Yet, I enjoyed developing and building this model more than anything else I've ever done.

As you have already guessed, it was not just a whim – like hmmmmm what will I build next? It was more like realizing a childhood ambition of building a blasted Ford that would fly. Fords are funny. They grow on you. Sentimental like. When I was a kid they were the biggest, shiniest, noisiest things I knew. They didn't fly at thirty thousand feet, but stayed down among the treetops where kids could see them and wave at the passengers and, who knows, maybe the passengers waved back, even if they were hurtling along at a hundred miles an hour!

Don't ask me why I chose TAT or NC9606 – it must be something I remember from the past, but I chose that particular plane . . .'

Even if a plane is entirely suitable as a subject for exact scale modelling, it will not be easy to reproduce in miniature form unless full and authentic information can be obtained about the prototype, and unless this is subjected to the closest possible scrutiny (nothing can lower a scale modeller's morale more rapidly than being told by an observant critic that the serial numbers on his masterpiece are upside down, or that its international markings just do not make sense).

Far left – A fine scale model of S.E. 5a built by Gerald Wingrove. It is detailed down to the spark plugs, made of brass and covered in silk.

Left – A close-up view of the cockpit and gun mounting in Wingrove's model S.E. 5a

Above – Wingrove's model S.E. 5a in course of construction

The book *Jane's All the World's Aircraft* is an excellent source of reference, but the drawings and diagrams in it, though admirably accurate, may not be sufficiently detailed for the modeller's purposes. However, the address of the manufacturer of the chosen plane can normally be found in *Jane's*.

Providing photographs and plans for aeromodellers is not always a very rewarding occupation for airplane manufacturers – they make their profits, if any, from considerably larger deals. Some firms do allow their Public Relations Departments to supply information of the sort aeromodellers require – they regard this as a useful form of advertisement – but others recommend enquirers to apply to one of the well-known plan companies such as (in Britain) the *Aeromodeller* Plans Service and (in America) the 'Sudden Service' project of the *American Aircraft Modeler*.

Many great public museums, such as the Science Museum at South Kensington, London and the Imperial War Museum at Lambeth in the same city, offer splendid opportunities for study by the serious scale modeller. To take an outstanding American example: the Smithsonian's National Air and Space Museum at Washington, D.C., has many historic and record-breaking aircraft on permanent display and others frequently appear there on loan. Complete photo coverage and authentic plans for the original planes are in the museum files, and copies can be obtained for nominal charges. The museum's officials are as helpful to aero-

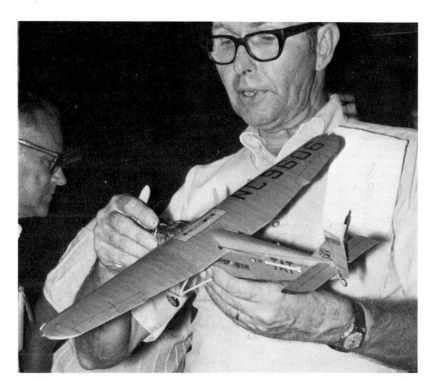

93 Left above – Fulton Hungerford with his classic Ford Trimotor scale model

94 Left below – Sub-assemblies used in the construction of Hungerford's Ford model

modellers as the unceasing calls on their services allow them to be.

Nostalgia is an emotion enjoyed now by many scale modellers – in the world of model aircraft, as well as in the worlds of model trains and of model ships and boats. To satisfy the needs of these backward-looking craftsmen, many of whom demand precise and recondite data about the machines that flew in World Wars 1 and 2, some very efficient and up-to-date organizations have been set up. One of the most effective of these specialized societies – the 'Cross and Cockade' – was formed on a non-profit-making basis in the United States in 1959 so that all who had a common interest in the history of aviation in the 1914–18 period could share their information and knowledge. Membership of the society increased rapidly, and now there are associates, modelling the relatively primitive aircraft of this era and winning important awards with their work, in virtually all parts of the world.

Even with all these sources of information to tap, an aeromodeller wanting to make an exact scale model may find that his researches have to be considerably extended. When Fulton Hungerford set out to build his classic Ford model, he had half a file drawer 'full of Ford photos, clippings and stuff' from which he made up a loose leaf binder of material that was applicable to the NC 9606. But there were still some mysteries to be solved. Hungerford later recorded:

'. . . I wasn't sure about the colors. Was TAT painted over the door on 9606 as it showed on photos of 9650? And so on. I wrote TWA (Trans-World Airlines), the Smithsonian (Institution), *Model Airplane News*, the *New York Times*, the American Aviation Historical Society and, finally the AAHA gave me Bill Larkin's address. That man is a gold mine of information on the Fords. He sent me no less than a dozen 8 × 10s of Fords, and most of them were 9606. The door was not at the last window like most other Fords, but at the next-window-forward position. To my knowledge, that is the only Ford 5-AT with the door in the 4-AT position . . .'

5 Hungerford's Ford model ready
or flight

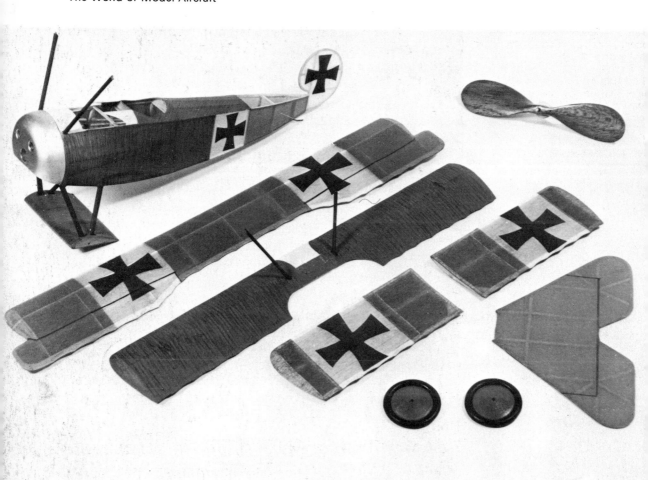

96 Above — The principal components of the model Fokker triplane shown on page 104

97 Left — A scale model of a notorious dive bomber, the Junkers Ju 87 *Stuka*

98 Right — A miniature pilot correct to scale. This tiny figure was carved from balsa.

99 and 100 Below — Two stages in the production of a three-bladed propeller carved from a composite block of balsa

101 Below, right — A scale model Nieuport 28 designed for free-flying purposes

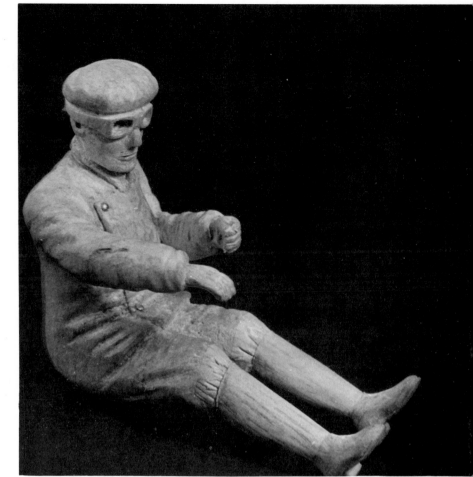

If a scale model airplane is intended, when it has been completed, to stand still and to be admired, it can be made from materials such as balsa and polystyrene that are comparatively easy to shape and do not have to be especially light or especially strong. But however accurate it may be in its outlines and general configuration, no scale model, static or flying, will win many awards for the realistic representation of a prototype unless its maker takes a lot of care with the many small and apparently insignificant details that have to be added to the principal components. The regulations formulated by the officials of the AMA for the appraisal of flying scale outdoor models powered by rubber state that the judging of static details should include such items as the wing, tail and landing gear rigging (struts, wires, etc.); windscreens, canopies, windows, doors etc.; control surfaces with such details as horns and cables; engines with their cowls, exhausts, etc.; and exterior 'instruments' such as antennas, generators, lights, pitot tubes, stall horns and fuel gauges. The exterior 'fittings' they recommend judges to look at include steps, walks, handles, fuel caps, hatches and plates; armament guns, bombs, rockets, flares and ammunition; identification markings such as insignias and registration numbers; and placards and signs in general or specific aircraft colouring. How do the judges know if the modeller has carried out his intention faithfully? Usually, the onus is on the competitor, who may be required to produce the photographs or drawings from which he has been working.

Sometimes, a modeller attempting to make a true-to-scale replica of some part of a plane's equipment may be faced with apparently insuperable problems. The wheels fitted to aircraft in the years prior to 1918 (for example) were made in almost every case with wire spokes that fitted into circular rims – rather like the wheels of the modern pedal bicycle. Uncovered spoked wheels of this kind are extremely difficult to construct on a very small scale, and most model-makers would find it quite impossible to imitate the prototypes exactly. However, the wheels found on present-day planes have, almost invariably, plain conical sections, and are fitted with tyres with relatively large diameters. Small-scale versions of these modern wheels are quite easily made with papier mâché or glass fibre – some modellers use plaster of paris moulds to form their contours. A careful craftsman can easily draw or paint lines and spots on one of these relatively plain modern wheels so that it resembles a pre-1918 vintage wheel over which fabric covers have been fitted. (These covers, laced to the rim on both sides of the wheel, were intended to prevent mud collecting between the spokes, which would have added disastrously to the weight of the comparatively primitive machine.) Only the very keenest and most critical observers will be able to spot this little deception.

Scram, a rubber-powered model at an old-time meet

Overleaf, a museum model of the Fiat MF4 flying boat

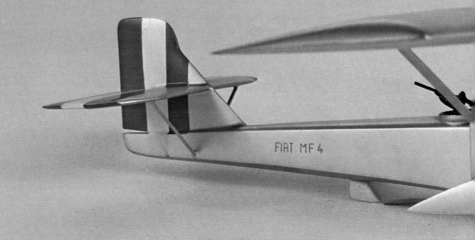

If a scale model airplane is intended to fly – and there is no more inspiring sight in the whole world of model aircraft than that of a perfectly detailed miniature plane emulating exactly the performance of its full-sized prototype – some very special difficulties have to be overcome.

To begin with, one of the most important factors that have to be considered: in a real, full size airplane there will normally be a live, thinking pilot aboard. A model, necessarily, is pilotless. Where the prototype has been designed to fulfil some specific purpose – as, for example, if it is a combat fighter that is required to roll and turn with maximum manoeuvrability – it will have some unusual characteristics in its conformation. So, a prototype combat fighter will probably have little or no wing dihedral and it is almost certain to have a relatively large vertical tail. A free-flying scale model that reproduces these characteristics exactly is likely to be 'spirally unstable' – that is, having no pilot aboard handling the controls and able to supply continual correction – it will be dangerously liable to roll off into a spiral dive from which it has very little chance of pulling out. So, certain compensating adjustments have to be made if a 'true-to-prototype' scale model of this fighter is to be freely flown without disaster. And the same limitation applies to the vast majority of flying scale models.

To find out what deviations from the prototype will have to be made in each case, a certain amount of trial flying will be necessary. Fulton Hungerford, a member of the launch team due to land the first men on the moon, was prevented by this big event from taking his Ford Trimotor model to the 1969 National Championships as he had planned. With an extra year to strive for perfection, he was able to carry out some additional research. Here are some notes he made about the second version he constructed:

'It will fly level, and with about half power, make the smoothest landings you ever saw! I mean, really. A touchdown so easy and gentle that the wheels touch and start rolling, then the shocks take up part of the weight of the plane, and it settles easily – but that's with half power. If you try to glide it, it comes in *hard* at a thirty degree angle. I did a lot of experimenting with that model. Built no less than five stabilizers. One was 1·25 larger area: the next 1·50, etc., finally in desperation I built one with one-half the area of the wing. All the same. Thirty degree angle, with the nose and landing gear touching the ground at the same time. I went back to the scale size elevator . . .'

But why is all this punctiliousness necessary? One might think that even without a pilot on board, a miniature plane based on a proven and fairly orthodox prototype, and reproducing that proto-

above, a scratch-built plastic-
rd scale model of a Sopwith
p
elow, a rubber-powered scale
odel of a *Gee Bee* racer built
om a Cleveland kit

type exactly in every detail, should perform just as effectively in its own little way as the full-sized plane. Unfortunately, the world of model aircraft is far from being as straightforward as that. Something rather vital tends to get lost in the process of scaling down, and further adjustments have to be made to any small scale flying model to compensate for this lessening in efficiency.

Small-scale wings, for instance, are unlikely to provide the amount of lift necessary to keep a model in the air unless their proportions are changed considerably. To understand why this should be so, one has to consider the 'airfoil section' – the shape that would result if a clean cut were made with a sharp knife through the wing in a direction exactly parallel to the fore-and-aft centre line of the plane.

To provide lift, the upper surface of a wing has to be curved more noticeably than its lower surface. When the air molecules are parted by the wing's leading edge, the molecules travelling the greater distance over the upper surface of the wing will have to move much faster than those passing below the under surface if all are to meet up and combine again in harmony behind the wing's trailing edge. If this happens properly, the air pressure on the upper surface is reduced, while the air pressure on the lower surface remains constant or is increased. So, the required forces result, or should result.

Clearly, if the chord or effective width of a wing is reduced from ten or twelve feet to five or six inches, the air molecules' chance to adjust and re-adjust themselves will be proportionately lessened. Even if the wing of the model is tilted to the oncoming airflow at a greater angle than it is in the prototype, so that the air striking the lower surface of the wing will exert some extra pressure and will help to push the wing skywards the compensation may not be sufficient. So, the ultra-reliable 'Clark Y' airfoil, which has a completely flat lower surface and provides lift at a very wide range of angles and airspeeds, has usually to be adopted for all working scale models except the very fastest. If, by this departure from the actual dimensions of the original, the appearance of the model is made to differ too radically from that of the prototype, the change has to be disguised, to the greatest possible extent, when the outside surfaces are painted.

Another, and most important, component of an airplane may be its propeller (if it is that kind of an aircraft). Unfortunately, a true-to-scale miniature propeller fitted to an exactly correct model airframe is likely to be quite inadequate, since the limited chord of the blade will not drive air in a rearward direction with sufficient power to move the model forward at the necessary speed. A propeller with blades that will do the job efficiently may look much too big and clumsy for the model. Once again, there has to be some

102 A scale flying model made from balsa and other materials in course of assembly

103 Below – One of the finest flying scale models ever marketed the radio-controlled Ryan STA Special, designed by Maxey Hester

form of compromise. So, in most flying scale model contests, propellers are considered only for their practical qualities and are not judged for their scale truth to the prototype. Ready-made plastic or wooden propellers are usually allowed in these contests, but they are not awarded points for workmanship or finish.

True-to-scale model aircraft have been used on innumerable occasions for wind tunnel research. In one of these tunnels, an even flow of air at a controlled speed is provided by powerful fans

104 A flying scale model of a well-loved prototype – the Gloster *Gladiator*

and a scale model of the plane being studied, or of the projected plane, is suspended in the moving airstream. (Although the model is stationary, virtually the same effects are produced as if it were moving in still air.) Scale models placed in wind tunnels are often hung upside-down so that they may be the more easily connected to the instruments used to measure the forces experienced by the model. Complicated calculations are necessary before the results obtained from the tests can be interpreted in terms that are applicable to full-sized aircraft.

If the aircraft is intended to fly at supersonic speeds, similar tests will probably be carried out in a special supersonic wind tunnel. Because a great deal of power is required to run such a tunnel, it is generally much smaller than a subsonic wind tunnel and so the models used in it have to be smaller and must be constructed with the greatest possible accuracy.

Many people would like to make exact scale replicas of classic airplanes without having to devote an enormous amount of time to research and without having to shape too many of the parts from scratch. Just by buying a commercially produced kit and assembling the components, an ambitious modeller, who realizes his own limitations, can look forward to owning a stunning replica, with a six-foot wing span, of the world famous Ryan STA Special. Each kit, offered by the Sig Manufacturing Company of Montezuma, Iowa, contains a sufficient quantity of high grade balsa for the structure and planking; die-cut formers and ribs; a large instruction manual with 100 isometric views, and photographs, which make it easy for the modeller to carry out each process in the construction of the plane; forty-three ready formed plastic parts, which include the engine cowling, the landing gear, the fairing, the wheel spats, the air scoops, the pilot's head rest, and various streamline covers. All the instrument dials and cockpit placards are reproduced photographically so that they will be exactly to scale and will resemble, as closely as possible, those in the prototype. A model made to these specifications by Maxey Hester took second place in the 1970 radio-controlled scale model World Championships.

Having made a true-to-scale model aircraft of any merit, any normally proud craftsman will want to take photographs of it, or to have photographs taken, stressing its 'reality'. Here again, problems are likely to arise that result directly from the reduction in size of the subject. When a full scale prototype aircraft is photographed, the apparent convergence of parallel straight lines (perspective) will be accurately recorded by the camera. This will give the viewer a true idea of the relative size and depth of the various parts of the plane. If a small model of the same plane is photographed with the same camera, the lack of perspective will indicate clearly, in the finished record, that the subject is only inches long, instead of many feet. To counteract this tendency, a wide-angle lens with or without a close-up attachment can sometimes be substituted for the lens normally used with the camera. A carefully chosen photographic background can be placed behind a scale model, too, to help to produce the illusion that the little aircraft is the real thing.

Occasionally, true-to-scale model aircraft have been used by film makers and the producers of television programmes to represent full-sized prototypes. In May 1971, for example, four-engined, fully radio-controlled models of the Avro *Lancaster* bomber were flown at West Malling, to the South of London, so that films made of them while they were in the air could be included in the British Broadcasting Corporation's 'Pathfinders' video series. Each model weighed 28 pounds and had a wing span of eleven feet. Operating at ranges of up to half a mile, and at altitudes up to 500 feet, the models were flown, so that they would produce the most dramatic visual effects, in sessions that started soon after sunset and lasted until just before dawn, searchlights being used to provide the necessary illumination. When, at a press viewing, one of the models came prematurely to earth, the incident was reported in the following morning's *Daily Express* under the nostalgic and arresting headline 'ONE OF OUR AIRCRAFT IS MISSING'.

7 Model Aircraft Powered with Internal-combustion Engines

Shortly before the outbreak of World War 1, enthusiasts in several different parts of the world were experimenting with model aircraft engines driven by the fuel known as gasoline (in America) and as petrol (in Britain and some other English-speaking countries).

An Englishman named David Stanger was possibly the most successful of these innovators. One of Stanger's models – a tractor monoplane that looked very like one of Blériot's full-sized aircraft – is said to have made in 1914, a number of noteworthy flights. It is difficult to see how this happened, for the model had no dihedral or any other device for obtaining lateral stability, but the flights may have been made in abnormally calm weather.

Stanger's second machine – a tail-first biplane – was of more lasting interest. This model was 50 inches long and had a wing span of 7 feet. The power was supplied by a two-cylinder V-type gasoline engine that drove a 22-inch diameter propeller at 2,000 revolutions per minute. The weight of the model, complete, was $10\frac{3}{4}$ pounds, and its flying speed was estimated at 20 m.p.h. On one celebrated day also in 1914 at the Royal Aero Club at Hendon in North West London this model made history by making an officially observed flight of 51 seconds – easily a world record at that time. For this remarkable achievement Mr. Stanger was awarded the enormous sum of £10. He was not much troubled by potential rivals, for none of the other entrants for the competition for power-driven models even qualified to start.

Mr. Stanger's supremacy was not seriously challenged until 1931, when two or more gasoline-powered models were displayed and tested at the American National Contests at Dayton, Ohio. In the same year, Carl Carlson of Chicago entered a gasoline-powered model plane for a record event. The plane had a span of 11 feet and weighed $9\frac{1}{2}$ pounds. Unfortunately it crashed shortly after taking off, so no new record was established.

In the following year, Lieutenant-Colonel C. E. Bowden, who was an Associate of the Institute of Mechanical Engineers (in Britain), decided to cut down the amount of time he was spending on the construction of rubber-powered model aircraft and to

95 An early gasoline model. Appropriately called *Goliath*, this plane had a 9-foot wing-span. It was designed by G. W. W. Harris and built and flown by Arthur Fox.

devote the hours he saved to the design and production of a gasoline-driven machine that could be used for general purpose flying. To achieve this object, Colonel Bowden planned to build a model of reasonable size that could be taken to pieces easily, re-erected quickly, and carried in an automobile. He decided, too, to avoid over-rigidity of construction and to make his model as crash-proof as possible by keeping its component parts in position with absorbent rubber fixings. The smallest engine he could find find was an old but stout 28 cubic centimetre 'Wall' two-stroke taken from a model speedboat that belonged to his friend Edgar T. Westbury. The Dunlop Rubber Company sportingly made two special wheels to the Colonel's requirements, and Mr. (later, Sir) Richard Fairey kindly allowed him to use the beautifully flat expanses of the Fairey Aviation Company's aerodrome near Heathrow.

The Colonel named the biplane model that resulted from all this activity after the mother kangaroo called *Kanga* in A. A. Milne's stories, since he hoped that it would hop when required! His wishes were granted on a summer Sunday afternoon when *Kanga* set up a new world record for gasoline-driven free flight in the open air, recording – among other good times – one flight of 71 seconds. A film of the machine was made by *Pathétone Weekly*, and, largely as a result of the publicity it received, the production of power-driven model aircraft rapidly developed into a world-wide movement.

Enthusiasts in the United States showed particularly keen interest in the exciting new pastime, and soon small engines suitable for use in model aircraft were being manufactured there in very large numbers. The 9 cubic centimetre 'Brown Junior' engine, developed in 1934 by William Brown of the Junior Motors Corporation of Philadelphia, Pennsylvania was outstandingly successful – so much so, that the company was able to issue an offset news bulletin called the *Brown Junior Motor News*.

By 1936, it had been reported that an 8-foot span model monoplane built by the American Maxwell Bassett and powered with one of the original Brown motors had flown from the Central Airport, Camden, New Jersey, to Middletown, Delaware – a distance of some 70 miles. This famous flight lasted for two and a half hours, the maximum altitude reached by the model being 8,000 feet.

The 'Brown Junior' was soon followed by the equally famous 6 cubic centimetre 'Baby Cyclone', and these two small, light American engines were for a number of years among the best commercially obtainable. From Canada, there came the tiny 2·3 cubic centimetre 'Elf' which ran with remarkable smoothness but, understandably, lacked the kind of power that is expected

Dick Graham's home-built radio-controlled model of the *Liberty Sport*

today. Outstanding in his efforts to popularize gasoline-model activities at this time was Nathan Polk, Director of the Newark branch of Polk's Modelcraft Hobbies, who was one of the first men anywhere in the world to sponsor competitions between the new powered planes.

In 1936, the International Gas Model Airplane Association was organized by Charles H. Grant, Editor of the American *Model Airplane News*. (His magazine carried the only column devoted entirely at that time to gasoline models: it was called 'Gas Lines'.) By 1937, Grant claimed that his Association had 3,000 members. It had clubs in most cities, such as the Philadelphia Gas Model Association; the Boston Gas Model Society; the Gas Model Airplane Association of Southern California; the Gas Bugs of Rockford, Illinois; the Quaker City Gas Model Airplane Club; and many more.

Then, the movement began to run into serious trouble.

The high-pitched and insistent noise of a small gasoline motor can be intensely annoying to those whose interests do not extend to the public operation of model aircraft. With thousands of novice fliers proudly trying out their new powered craft from every available garden, park and school yard this noise, in America, quickly rose to a nearly deafening crescendo. Worse, the freely flying machines were liable to land unexpectedly in inconvenient places, causing unforeseen damage and (occasionally) discomfort to the unaware. Soon, opposition to the new type of flying model became vocal, and general. The Department of Commerce, aware of the high feelings that had been aroused, considered a ban on the free flying of model aircraft with gasoline motors. Two states – Connecticut and Massachusetts – actually put such a ban into effect, declaring that gas model flying was an illegal menace to personal and private property, and that those who practised the hobby were introducing serious new hazards into the home and were endangering the full-sized aircraft who had more right to the skies.

Very active, at this time, was an association of aeromodellers known as the Junior Birdmen of America. Sponsored by the huge Hearst newspaper chain, and aided by all the publicity that such a great organization can provide for its protegés, the Junior Birdmen claimed, in 1937, that they had a national membership of 467,852. They ran their own local and national championship contests every year, with many fine cups and trophies for prizes, and it was believed that the officials of this happy band were eager to take over the control of competitive aeromodelling in the United States, on a national scale.

When the opposition to gasoline-powered models became fierce, however, these ambitious officials made a fatal blunder.

ove, a fine power model at the
orld Championships in Austria

low, the Russian power-model
am at the 1967 World Champion-
ips in Czechoslovakia

106 Left — David Stanger's tail-first model biplane, which established a world record in 191

107 A close-up of a CO_2 engine installed in a scale model Heinkel He 46. This engine was designed by the American, William Brown, who was the maker of the first commercially produced integral combustion engine for model aircraft.

Instead of trying to move with the times, they carried out, in the Hearst newspapers, a prolonged campaign that was intended to encourage still more flying with rubber-powered models, and to discredit entirely their new gasoline-powered rivals. Charles Grant, aided by sympathetic officials of the National Aeronautic Association and of the newly formed Academy of Model Aeronautics, quickly launched an effective counter-campaign, which was also backed by extensive publicity. Largely as a result of Grant's skilful and tenacious advocacy, the men of the Department of Commerce altered their avowed intention to ban the flying of gasoline-powered models and, instead, they issued an unequivocal statement in which they vouched for the value, to the youth of America, of the vigorous new extension of aeromodelling. The Association of Junior Birdmen thereupon completely and finally disintegrated.

Unaffected by the pro- and anti-gasoline engines struggle, a number of aeromodellers had been quietly – literally, quietly – producing model aircraft powered by compressed air. There were even events included for these, in a few contests. The engines could be bought ready-made, in kit form, or they could be constructed from plans published in the books and magazines of the period. Occasional experiments are made with compressed air model aircraft engines, even today. 'All you need is a tire pump (and you probably need the exercise)' claimed one compressed air advocate, recently:

During World War 2, the use of petrol for model aircraft engines was generally frowned on, and actually forbidden in several countries. In the United States, the AMA headquarters became suddenly like the main office of a gasoline rationing board. Letters poured in from desperate modellers requesting ration cards,

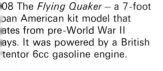
108 The *Flying Quaker* – a 7-foot span American kit model that dates from pre-World War II days. It was powered by a British Mentor 6cc gasoline engine.

letters of authorization, or information on where the precious fuel could be obtained. Of course, the Academy's officials were unable to do more than recommend that each individual modeller should go before a local rationing board with a request for sympathetic consideration. By July 1942, letters were being received from grateful gas-model fliers announcing their success in obtaining the small quantities of fuel necessary for carrying on their activities for six months or more. Early in 1943 it was officially decreed that American gasoline rationing regulations would permit modellers to keep their aircraft in the air as long as humanly possible. In spite of this, many daunting difficulties remained.

Work with 'gassies' – the word is derived from gasoline – soon revived after the ending of hostilities, and the rapid development of the miniature diesel engine (favoured principally in Europe) and of the glowplug engine (particularly on the American side of the Atlantic Ocean) increased international interest in powered models of all kinds. In the older type of petrol engine, an electric spark had been used to ignite the charge at the plug, and even the most successful modellers had tended to regard occasional engine troubles as inescapable hazards of their hobby. One of the greatest advantages of both glowplug engine and the miniature diesel is their reliability.

The glowplug engine operates in exactly the same way as an engine of the older type, except for its means of ignition. Instead of being fired by an electric spark, the charge in one of the newer engines is ignited by a glowing coil of wire. To start an engine of this kind, it is necessary to use a battery that will heat the element sufficiently to make it glow. In the early days of glowplug ignition, comparatively heavy batteries had to be used for this, but small light nickel-cadmium cells were soon developed that will supply the amperes necessary for a number of glowplug starts and can be re-charged many times. Once an engine fired by a glowplug has started to run, the starting battery may be disconnected, as the heat of the combustion in the engine will be sufficient to keep the wire in the glowplug at the temperature required for further ignition.

The design of glowplug engines produced commercially for model aircraft has become increasingly sophisticated in recent years as competition in the industry has increased. To attract a sufficient number of customers to make the manufacture of one of these engines profitable, the engine offered has to be light, compact and powerful; it has to be as vibration-free as possible, or it will tend to shake apart all the glue joints in the model to which it is fitted; it must not cause radio failure, at any speed; and it must be capable of 'idling down' to a point at which it is really doing little more than ticking over. It is remarkable how many engines satisfy all these requirements and manage to be surprisingly inexpensive

109 A model of a high-wing cabin aircraft with a wing span of 48 inches. Powered by an E.D. Bee 1cc engine, the plane was constructed by Anthony Hutchings of Petersfield, England, when he was 14. After 24 years, and having been lost on numerous occasions, the model is still fully operational. It has flown, free-flight, at least 600 times.

110 Right – A McCoy .049 cubic inch glowmotor. This versatile engine is equally at home in control-line, free-flight or single-channel radio-controlled models

111 Far right – An O.S. Max-H 60F glowplug engine used for radio-controlled models. This good stock engine is shown with a silencer attached

as well. Firms such as Gordon Burford and Co. Ltd, of Henley Beach, South Australia, who make the well-known 'Taipan' range of model aircraft engines; ETA Instruments Ltd, of Watford, England; and the brothers Cipolla of Trezzano, Italy add considerably to their countries' export figures, and there are many more.

The diesel engine is often called, more informatively, the 'compression-ignition engine'. In this kind of engine, no fire needs to be introduced into the cylinder, as the charge used – a mixture of an exceptionally volatile fuel, with air – can have its temperature raised to ignition point by being sufficiently compressed. With such abnormally high pressures to withstand, the diesel engines designed for use in model aircraft tend to be bulkier and heavier than spark-ignition and glowplug engines. But, they are powerful and easily operated, and will drive any models to which they are

112 A control-line scale model of an American Bendix racer powered by a large glowmotor

13 Right – A Dumas Products'
i-Lo model. Not being to scale,
this can have its engine exposed.

fitted for an exceptional distance or for every unit of fuel they consume. So, they are often preferred for competition models that are intended for such categories as team racing, where the economical use of fuel is all-important.

The fuels used for providing power for model aircraft today are normally made up with more care than the mixtures of gasoline and heavy mineral oil which were thought to be good enough for the early spark-ignition engines. For glowplug engines, fuels based on methanol – a form of alcohol – usually have castor oil (either natural or artificial) added to act as a lubricant, and other sub-

14 A Davies-Charlton Super
Merlin .76cc diesel engine

stances may be incorporated to help the methanol and castor oil to mix, to help an engine to start more easily, to produce more revolutions per minute, or for some other reason that the operator thinks is important. An enterprising modeller who wishes to get the greatest possible amount of power from an engine will often make a fuel to his formula to suit the conditions of temperature and humidity prevailing on one particular day or at one particular hour. Competitors who take their power-driven models to international contests will often find that standard mixtures of methanol and castor oil are supplied by the sponsors, and that the use of these fuels is insisted upon.

Much thought has to be given to the problems posed by the storage of the necessary fuel in fast model aircraft fitted with high-powered internal combustion engines and by the need to feed the fuel satisfactorily, with as constant a pressure as possible, to the engine(s). Tanks in a wide variety have been designed to suit models of each of the different types. In the wedge-shaped tank, for instance, which was developed primarily for control-line models, the fuel is driven by centrifugal force into the pointed end of the wedge, which is positioned on the side of the model furthest from the centre of the flying circle. Air-vent tubes attached to the lower as well as the upper surfaces of a tank of this kind ensure that

115 A free-flight scale model of a De Havilland D.H.2 powered with a CO_2 engine. Not a true internal combustion engine, the gas actuates the engine without combustion.

6 A close-up view of the nose an ingenious steam-powered odel

when the model turns over on its back while stunting, the engine will perform as well as if the plane is right side up. Other ingenious designs include tanks made from coiled lengths of tubing (the capacities of these are carefully assessed so that the periods of time the engines are to run may be exactly determined, the engines stopping immediately the fuel is exhausted); 'clunk' and 'clank' tanks fitted with flexible or rotating pickup tubes to ensure a consistent fuel feed, however a model is manoeuvred; and 'balloon' tanks which, as their name implies, conveniently decrease in size as the fuel they contain is withdrawn.

The problems caused by the noise made by model aircraft engines have still not been finally solved. In Britain, the officials of the SMAE, alarmed by the loss through complaints of a number of flying sites, have insisted that all the society's members who wish to take part in their officially-sanctioned competitions shall fit silencers or mufflers to engines that produce the harsh high-pitch sounds of lively exhausts, and the authoritative bodies of several other European countries have made regulations intended to save those who are not enamoured of the engine noise of model aircraft. The American AMA, unwilling to take really drastic action unless it becomes inescapable, has set up a 'muffler committee' to conduct a study of the technical aspects of noise abatement. Much progress has been made, but so far no engine-muffler has been manufactured that will not reduce, by a small percentage at least, the performance of the model to which it is fitted.

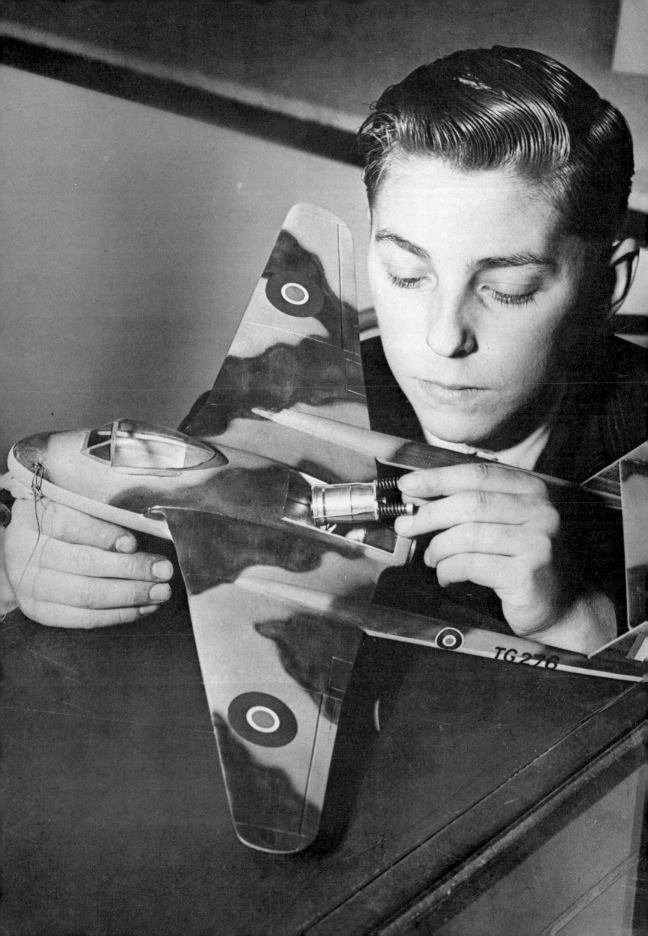

8 Jet-powered Model Aircraft

Frank Whittle, an Englishman born in 1907, was almost certainly the first person ever to exploit the possibilities of the gas turbine for the jet propulsion of aircraft. Whittle had been flying conventional propeller-driven model airplanes since he was four years old. When he left school at the age of sixteen, he joined the Royal Air Force as a boy apprentice. Three years later, he was awarded a cadetship at the Royal Air Force College at Cranwell, in Lincolnshire. There, he learned to fly, becoming, later, a pilot of outstanding qualities.

It was while he was serving at Cranwell that Whittle first became conscious of the limitations of speed and height that reduced the effectiveness of the orthodox propeller-driven plane with a piston-type engine. So, he sought for a more efficient method of propulsion. Soon, he had designed an engine which had an air intake at the front. By using a gas turbine that turned a kind of rotary fan, Whittle arranged that the air drawn in would be first compressed by the fan and then moved forcibly into a combustion chamber. Here, some liquid fuel such as kerosene would be sprayed into it and ignited. The compressed air, further expanded by the heat that resulted from the combustion of the fuel, would be expelled violently through an opening at the back of the combustion chamber. As it went past the blades of the turbine, it would make them rotate like the sails of a windmill. On leaving the turbine, the hot vapours would travel backwards in a powerful jet, producing, thereby, the strong forward thrust that Whittle had worked with so much ingenuity to create.

In 1930, Whittle took out the famous patent that was to protect his gas-turbine aero engine. In 1934, he went to study at Cambridge University so that he could learn enough to put his ideas into practice. Shortly after this, a company was formed to help him with his researches, and by 1937 the first Whittle engine had been built and was being tested on the ground.

In Germany, meanwhile, two men – Hans van Ohain and Max Hahn, who knew nothing of Whittle's work – had invented at roughly the same time an engine that worked in approximately the

7 The first jet engine for toys
s demonstrated at an Oxford
eet, London, store in 1948. A
ung technician fits one of the
y engines into a model *Vampire*
this historic occasion.

Left – A museum model of Gloster E 28/39 – the first ish jet-propelled aircraft

Left, below – A wind tunnel del used for aerodynamic earch at the American National onautics and Space ministration

Above left – A Jetex 50 tor and (above right) a Jetex A Loader

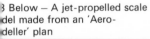

Above and (122) right – A Kraft duration model with ex 50 motor in position

Below – A jet-propelled scale del made from an 'Aero-deller' plan

same way as his. A plane powered by one of their engines did actually get off the ground on the 27th August 1939, but it was really Whittle's British Government-sponsored experimental prototype – the Gloster E28/39 – which flew on the 15th May 1941, that heralded an entirely new age in the history of aeronautics. Whittle personally piloted this plane in most of its trial and proving flights. Soon, *Meteor* aircraft of various marks were in production in the Gloster Aircraft Company's Gloucestershire factory.

Very shortly after the full-sized, jet propelled planes had been seen by members of the general public and the full significance of their lack of propellers had been properly appreciated, an entirely new principle was introduced into the design of model planes.

Obviously, Whittle's engines could not be exactly reproduced, one hundred times or so smaller. But, model-makers learned quickly the lessons that Whittle could teach them. Propulsion in models that represent jet-powered aircraft, they saw, could be provided by any properly contrived little unit that would exert extra pressure in a forward direction by lessening the pressure at its rear. (One authority has likened this to the performance of an inflated rubber balloon that has suddenly had its input tube untied.) Contrary to popular belief, a jet-powered model does not manage to fly by shooting its engines' exhausts out aft to push against the air behind. It would work just as effectively in a vacuum.

Simple, and safe, are the 'Jetex' model jet engines, which were

124 Left – Len Ranson designed this successful jet-propelled model

125 Right – A flying scale model of the carrier-borne Hawker/Armstrong Whitworth *Sea Hawk* interceptor fighter

developed in Britain and are still, at the moment of writing, manufactured only there. The performance of a Jetex engine when ignited, though nearer to that of a rocket engine than to that of a true jet, is entirely appropriate for any medium-sized model aircraft that does not have to be obviously propeller-driven. The fuel makes a perceptible hissing noise, which is not so loud that the sound seems out of scale, and it emits a little (but not too much) smoke. As engines of this kind produce no torque effects whatever, they are eminently suitable for use with models that have a limited wing span. A model of a modern jet fighter for instance, may be ideally suited by a pair of Jetex engines.

Each Jetex engine consists of a small cylinder, which is sealed at one end. Covering the other end – placed to the rear of the aircraft – there is a removable cap. This cap has a small hole at its centre – and it is important that it should be kept small. If any implement that is too thick or abrasive is used for cleaning out the orifice, a serious lack of thrust in subsequent launchings may result.

Fuel is supplied for Jetex engines in the form of cylindrical pellets, made of a compressed powder that can be relied on to burn steadily and cannot possibly explode. The pellets are so harmless that they can be sent lawfully through the mails. Each engine is designed to accommodate two pellets – one pellet being sufficient for a flight of limited duration, or for a test run.

If a Jetex engine is fitted into a model built from a kit, great care

has to be taken to see that the directions provided by the manufacturers are followed exactly. Undoubtedly, their expert designers will have gone to a lot of trouble to see that the little engine can be accommodated as effectively and as safely as possible in the model, and their copy-writers will have been just as meticulously briefed. So, if the instruction sheet says that any part of the model should be covered with some material that will insulate it adequately from the heat generated by the engine, it would be unwise to ignore this warning. Asbestos paper is quite cheap, and is easy to fit.

If a Jetex engine is fitted into a model built to any other design, the following few points have to be carefully watched, or trouble may result:

The powerful thrust-producing exhaust must have an exit-passage that is completely free from interruption of any kind.

The engine should be sited in such a way that it has adequate cooling space around it.

The engine should be sited in such a way that the spent charges can be removed quickly and easily after each flight. After the engine has been thoroughly cleaned, it should be possible for replacement units to be slipped into the cylinder with equal speed and facility.

The engine should be fixed in position in such a way that the direction of its thrust can be altered slightly if the performance of the model, in its test flights, suggests that this may be necessary.

The engine should be sited and fixed in position in such a way that each flight can be started easily and safely.

The fuel, in a Jetex engine, is ignited by means of a thin fuse or wick, which is arranged so that it protrudes through the small central hole in the middle of the engine's removable cap. The fuses have to be handled with care. There is a very thin wire running through each which will keep the inflammable material from disintegrating completely, even if a small part of it happens to become broken, but there is no certainty that a damaged fuse will ignite a charge, so a careful inspection has to be made.

The fuses are more flexible when they are warm, so in cold weather they are often carried to flying grounds in containers kept in the operator's clothing. It may help if a fuse is held between the palms of the hands for a few moments before any attempt is made to coil it.

To keep the fuses pressed firmly against the surface of the fuel, gauze washers are provided, and these have to be kept clean. A discarded toothbrush is useful for this. The washers should be thrown away after they have been used – say – five times.

A display of model jet planes in the Fiat Museum

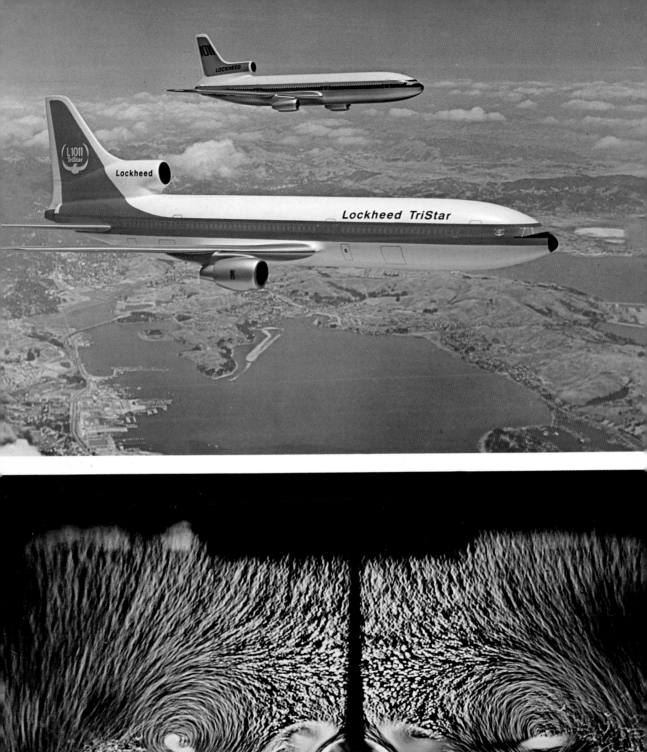

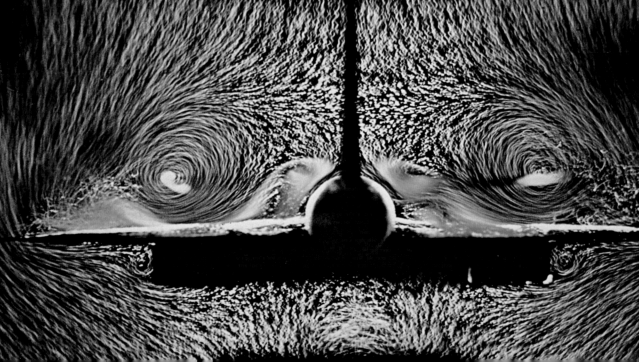

Usually, a lighted cigarette is enough to ignite the fuse. Conventional safety matches can be used, but they are liable to set fire to the model.

When a model aircraft powered with a Jetex engine, or engines, is being launched, care has to be taken to see that the model is carefully aligned and that the wind has not changed its direction. Once the lighted fuel has started to give off its first sibilant jet of gas, the model is normally held for two or three seconds more, so that the thrust can build up. (If it is released too soon, the model will probably be moving in an unwanted direction by the time the thrust starts to have its proper effect.) As soon as the engine has attained full power, the model is launched forward gently, much as a simple model glider is launched by hand. Momentarily, the model may then seem to hesitate, but it will soon accelerate, and within a few seconds it should be travelling forwards and upwards like a perfectly tuned prototype. When the plane lands, at the end of its flight, the Jetex engine is likely still to be very hot. A cautious operator will check that it is cool enough to touch before he attempts to handle it.

Some other jet engines – larger and more powerful than the 'Jetex' type units – are used occasionally in model aircraft, the Furrer (of Swiss origin), the Aristojet (from Germany), the O.S. (from Japan), the Vulcan (from Italy) and the Dynajet (from the United States) being arguably the best known.

The impressive American unit was developed by Sergeant William L. Tenney, from Minneapolis. Shortly after the end of World War 2, a number of German V 1 'Flying Bombs' of the type that had been flown against targets in Britain were shipped to the United States. One of these pilotless gyro-stabilized 'Doodlebugs' was sent to the American Air Force test centre at Wright Field, near Dayton, Ohio. While it was on display there, Tenney was able to examine it. Noting the jet reaction unit mounted externally, above the rear fuselage, Tenney decided to try his hand at making similar propulsion units, on a smaller scale, for use with model aircraft. His first attempt – made in association with Charlie Marks, of Las Vegas – was six feet long and weighed about 35 pounds. Clumsy as it was, it worked, and soon Tenney and Marks were able to put more refined versions into production. By 1953, they had sold several thousand.

Weighing almost exactly one pound, a typical Dynajet engine depends, for producing its thrust, on a valve made of thin sheet metal. The flow of air through an engine of this kind is started with a bicycle pump, a car foot pump, or with a compressed air line. With the air, a small amount of pure gasoline is taken in. The atomized mixture, fired by a sparking plug, explodes violently. The force of the explosion closes the valve momentarily, but it is

*bove, models of the Lockheed
iStar made for publicity
urposes

elow, vortices around the wings
* a model *Concorde* in a hydro-
namic tunnel

quickly re-opened by the next input of the mixture of fuel and air. After the cycle has been repeated a few times creating a 'pulse' the engine should start to operate by itself without any further assistance from the forced air input. When this happens, the recurrent explosions merge into a loud roar that is practically continuous and can be (to those not prepared for the noise) a little alarming. As the parts of the engine nearest to the combustion chamber are liable to become red hot, the uses of a power unit of this kind are necessarily limited.

The very high speeds attained by the American jet-powered models were soon rivalled by those of some European innovators. In Czechoslovakia, Zdeněk Husička produced his brilliant Letmo series of engines. (One of these, mounted on an asymmetrical model which had all its lifting surfaces on one side of the centre line, enabled him in May 1952 to lift the world speed record for a timed run to 153·157 m.p.h.) Michael Vassilchenko, of the Tusino Research Laboratories in Moscow and Ivan Ivannikov his fellow-countryman introduced further refinements in their RAM jet units which made even higher speeds possible. By 1965, the world speed record for models of this kind had been raised by the Italian Ugo Rossi to 193·1 m.p.h. Augmenter tubes – allowed by the authorities – are favoured by many pulse-engine operators aiming at extremely high speeds. These are bell-mouthed pipes which draw in cool air through their expanded front ends and then expel it again at the tail of the model so that it will mingle with the hot gases that are escaping from the engine, reducing their temperature and contributing noticeably to the engine's thrust. Other ducting devices that do not make use of combustion are also permitted.

The very high speeds attained by these powerful models make line control almost obligatory, and stringent safety precautions have to be taken. So, the regulations for competitive jet model flying formulated by the officials of the FAI the AMA and other controlling bodies impose some commonsense limitations. (The FAI rules require that a jet must not weigh more than 500 grams [1·1 pounds], and that the total weight of the model, with fuel, must not exceed 1 kilogram [2·2 pounds]. The American body insists that 'no control-line speed jet model shall have a flying weight of more than 4 pounds'.) Without these controls, models driven by ultra high power pulse units could become unpleasantly reminiscent of incendiary bombs.

26 Left above – An experimental profile model powered with a Jetex engine

27 Left – A fast flying model of a Boeing 707 powered by two jet-type engines

28 Above – Compact profile-type models of this kind can be powered with Jetex engines

9 Control-line Flying

The year 1911 saw what is now believed to have been the first captive flight ever made with a gasoline-driven model airplane. Two French brothers named Godfrey had managed to produce a small V-shaped twin-cylinder engine that worked satisfactorily, so they fitted it to a model of the famous *Antoinette* full-sized monoplane. They tried the model out, attached to a line that was tethered at the other end to a pole set in the ground, at the historic Vélodrome du Parc des Princes, in front of a large crowd. The model flew successfully for five complete laps, then the line broke and the model flew off wildly into some railings. The shock seems to have been too much for the brothers Godfrey, for though they were clearly so near achieving powered free flight, they did not make a second attempt. One of the spectators – a M. Suzor – was, however, so impressed by what he had seen that more than a quarter of a century later he managed to trace, and photograph, the engine that had driven this sensational model.

Tethered flying, in a simple form, was practised in many different parts of the world in the years between World Wars 1 and 2. In Britain, for instance, Round-the-Pole (RTP) flying kept large numbers of aeromodellers happily occupied during the long dark winter evenings. The aim of these captive flights was, invariably, duration. The models were light-weight, and rubber-driven, and no serious attempts were made at control. In spite of the limitations of RTP flying, however, its two great advantages over free flight became apparent – it needed less ground and it needed less air space. (A model could fly for several hundred yards without leaving the confines of a relatively small clubroom.) The time soon came for the commercial exploitation of this increasingly popular sport.

By using the phrase 'a control-line model', an aeromodeller is usually trying to describe a model aircraft which is guided by cords or wires attached to a handle held by the operator. A model aircraft of this kind is limited obviously to flying in arcs and circles around the person who is exercising control, but within this apparently restricted range all kinds of exciting manoeuvres can be carried out.

29 The finer points of a control-line model are admired at a meeting of the Three Kings Aeromodellers Club, Mitcham, Surrey, England.

130 How Victor Stanzel advertised his novel control-line model planes

131 Below — A Testors *Silver Wand* model trainer designed for control-line operation

32 'U-Control' — a sensational announcement

One of the shrewdest men to see the possibilities of control-line flying was Victor Stanzel, of Texas in the United States. Stanzel caught aeromodellers' attention in January 1940 with an advertisement headed '"G"-LINE FLYING'. In this historic public announcement, Stanzel offered for sale his 'Gas Powered Super Speed Planes Flown under Full Control', adding, to avoid any possible confusion with another new branch of the trade, 'Not radio controlled'.

Stanzel's 'super speed planes' were called, suggestively, 'Sharks'. They were neat, low-winged models that could be easily assembled from Stanzel kits. Each was intended to be connected by a single line to the end of a straight rod held, like a magician's wand, in the operator's hand. Stanzel had not chalked up a huge advance on the older, RTP operators. He had, though, managed to produce one interesting variation on the well-tried theme – a Stanzel control rod could be raised or lowered, at the whim of the operator, to affect the flying attitude of the model at the end of the line. The

133 A KeilKraft *Phantom Mite* model trainer with control-line apparatus clearly shown

Shark itself had rigid surfaces, incapable of adjustment, so the line had to act more as a stabilizer than as a means of direction. But, a most memorable start had been made.

The follow-up came quickly when, in the September of the same year, the American Junior Aircraft Company, of Portland, Oregon, advertised nationally a more sophisticated version of the 'G-line' method. American Junior called their system 'U-Control'. The ideas on which U-control was based were mostly provided by Nevilles E. Walker – known, still, to all his admirers who have survived from that time as 'Jim'.

Jim Walker had been carrying out his researches for quite some time. The *Fireball* he had created for the American Junior Aircraft Company was (according to the advertisement) almost crash-proof; could be flown anywhere – small or large space – any time – day or night, windy or calm; and would respond instantly to piloting from the ground. Owing to the semi-finished form of its kit, the *Fireball* could be made ready for flight in less than six hours. It could make power dives; it could loop the loop as many as twenty-seven times, consecutively; and, it could make perfect landings at the will of the operator.

This announcement, head-lined 'THE BIGGEST NEWS TODAY IN MODEL AVIATION!' had an electrifying effect on the model aircraft world. Soon after it appeared, the energetic New

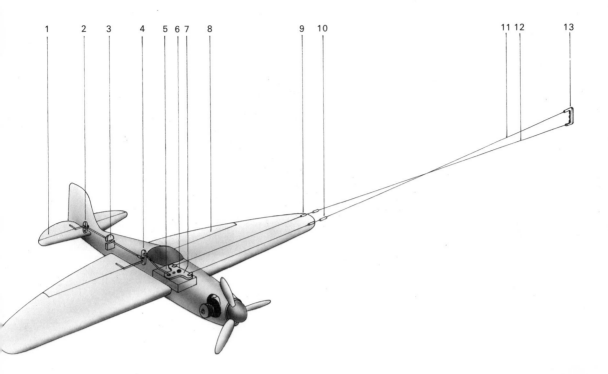

York model dealers Nat and Irwin Polk started to feature the *Fireball* in their influential promotion schemes; the Tiger Aero Company offered their engines as being the ideal power units for the American Junior models; and Jim Walker, in person, began stomping around the west coast districts of America giving displays of his new control-line techniques, inspiring, by doing this, many of those who saw him to follow his lead. In less than a year, all-*Fireball* speed and precision contests were being arranged.

The method developed by Walker was ingenious. Securely mounted in each of his model aircraft was a bellcrank – placed, usually, inside the fuselage or on the wing near the fuselage, according to the design of the model. This bellcrank pivoted freely around its attachment, and it had two long arms. To the end of each arm, Walker fastened a length of strong flexible wire that acted as a lead-out, passing through the wing, or under it, or over it, according (again) to the design of the model. At the free end of each lead-out, Walker made a loop, to which he attached one of his control lines. The other ends of the control lines were fastened to the two arms of a U-shaped handle which Walker (or one of his associates) held. When the operator pulled either wire, the bellcrank in the model turned in the required direction, and a pushrod attached at one end to the bellcrank and at the other to a control horn fixed on the elevator or elevator spar produced the desired effect. On

Boxing Day, 26th December 1940, Walker filed his famous Patent Application No. 2,292,416 ('Controlled Captive Type Toy Airplane') to protect his valuable invention. His drawings showed a third line, intended for engine speed control.

No one, in the world of model aircraft, is likely to remain content with any innovation, however startling, for very long. Soon, some skilled operators, impressed by Walker's virtuosity, began to experiment with involved control-line aerobatics and prolonged inverted (that is, 'upside down') flying. Within five years, stunt flying had become so popular in the territories through which Walker had passed that the Aeromodellers Association of Northern California were persuaded to draw up a schedule of aerobatics for contest purposes – probably, the first of such schedules in the whole history of aeromodelling. The movements required in this routine were: take off; fly on the level; climb; dive; wingover; make five inside loops; fly inverted; make one outside loop; execute a vertical figure of eight; carry out any extra manoeuvres not called for by the schedule; and land. Bonus points were to be awarded if the appearance of the model were especially noteworthy, and deductions were to be made if any of the operations included in the schedule were not successfully completed. Before long, aeromodellers' organizations in other parts of the world were to use this schedule as a basis on which to formulate their requirements for their own control-line contests.

It was a 12-year-old youth named Davis Slagle who first saw that any model required to fly belly-upwards for more than a few seconds would need a special kind of wing. By sticking two wings together, with their under surfaces touching, young Slagle produced a doubly thick wing which had a dual-purpose section. This juvenile prodigy carried off the 1947 American National Championships, and his spectacular achievements aroused much international interest in control-line flying.

The time was ripe for such a boom. The flying of model aircraft during World War 2 had been subject to severe restrictions in all the countries affected by hostilities. (Forbidden to use any type of fuel, most aeromodellers had had to revert, willy-nilly, to rubber-powered machines.) Released from these limitations, enthusiasts were desperately eager to make up for the years of lost time. Control-line flying – in which, apparently, even a juvenile could achieve supreme distinction – offered these frustrated people unprecedented opportunities to develop new skills and to earn world-wide fame. Before the year was out, aeromodellers in Britain, South Africa, and several other countries were striving to emulate, and even surpass, the feats of the pioneers in California.

Victor Stanzel of 'G-Line' fame, had not, in the meantime, been idle. In May 1947 he advertised some 'sensational new developments in control-line flying' (his own words). The most important novelties he was able to offer at this time were the 'Thum-It' precision control handle and the 'Control-It' precision elevator control unit. ('Comes completely assembled ready to be mounted in the fuselage of your model . . . $1.95'.) Neither of these gadgets did, in fact, sell in extraordinarily large numbers.

Stanzel did not have his really triumphant year until 1950, when, at the Chicago Model Trade Show he brought out his revolutionary new elevator control system, which required only a single line. Inviting all modellers to 'Fall in line with Mono-Line' Stanzel managed, by his ingenious innovation, to change the whole control line scene.

At its simplest, the mono-line control system is based on a handle designed to twist (rather than pull or release) the line. In the model, there is a spiral cam that is rotated by the turning line. A sliding follower attached to the cam operates the elevator, by means of a conventional push-rod. In models intended to fly at very high speeds, a worm cam – smaller and neater than a spiral cam – transmits the operator's intentions to the trimming mechanism.

What (all control-line enthusiasts asked at once) were the advantages of Stanzel's single wire method over the older, two-line U-Control? The Mono-Line's good points soon showed. In this system, there is no need for the line to be kept absolutely taut as the lines must be in the conventional Walker-type rig. Even when the line is quite slack, positive control can be applied to the trim of the machine just by moving the actuator at the pilot's handle forwards or backwards. And, Mono-Line has even greater advantage over U-Line: as the line resistance is so much less, higher flying speeds are possible. Five years after Stanzel introduced his new system, Mono-Line operators triumphed in nearly all the events at the United States National Trials, one small Mono-Line model flying at more than 100 m.p.h.

Today, speeds considerably higher than this are quite commonly recorded. The models intended to attain speed records are usually relatively small, and as they have to withstand a lot of engine vibration and the hazards of skid landings on hard concrete surfaces they have to be heavily built. Only the smallest control-line speed models are launched from the hand – larger machines are placed in wheeled cradles. (When the plane is travelling at sufficient speed to fly, it rises from the cradle and continues independently). The performance of a speed model is assessed by averaging the time it takes to fly a given number of laps. Speeds in excess of 190 m.p.h. have been recorded with machines in Class C (the Category that includes the largest speed models).

One of the most sophisticated hand control systems so far

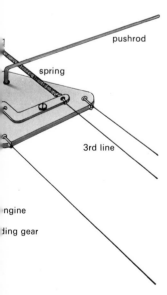

pushrod

spring

3rd line

ngine

ding gear

5 A diagram showing the use a second bellcrank for auxillary ntrols

136 A control-line combat mode
made from a balsa kit marketed
Messrs Pegasus

137 Below — A control-line scal
model of a De Havilland *Chipmu*
being refuelled

devised has been marketed by the J. Roberts Model Manufacturing Company, of Baker, Oregon, in the United States. In this system, three lines are used – two, to control the elevator of the model; the third, to make possible a full range of manoeuvres by allowing variable engine control at any stage in the model's circular orbit. Further refinements such as the operation of wheel brakes, landing flaps, and bomb bay doors can be introduced if some relatively simple alterations are made to the standard components.

Competitions for high-speed line-controlled model aircraft attract large entries now in almost every part of the world. (In Australia, for instance, the newer techniques have quelled practically all interest in traditional rubber-powered 'Wakefield' models). The AMA sanctions, at the present time, several different kinds of control line competition.

Speed events are popular with a great number of control line operators. In speed events covered by the AMA's regulations, no model is allowed to have a flying weight of more than four pounds. Control over the surfaces of the model that have to be manipulated during flight may be accomplished by mechanical means, or by electrical impulses transmitted through one or more of the lines.

Control-line endurance tests have as their stated objective: 'To fly a control-line model airplane powered by internal combustion reciprocating engine(s) so that it remains in the air for the greatest period of time.' Prolonged periods may be involved, the American Academy's officials warn in their handbook of regulations. For this reason, principally, endurance trials are not included in the schedules of many important events, where time is at a premium.

Team racing, on the other hand, provides an enormous amount of concentrated excitement at numbers of contests and is a real crowd-puller. In a team race, two or more models, each made correctly to specification, have to fly at the same time in the same circle over a pre-determined distance. All the competing models have to be started at the same time, the winner being the first to cover the required number of laps from a standing start. Stops for refuelling are, normally, mandatory in the course of each race. The skill of team members in this part of the operation is often decisive.

It is easy to see why team racing has become so popular in recent years, since it introduces into aeromodelling circles the fiercely competitive excitements of real air races. Fuel consumption has to be planned carefully against acceleration and speed, and pit stops have to be carried out with lightning efficiency, just as in the real-life sport. The most important factor is that the models look like real racers, and instead of competing one at a time against the stop watch, they can actually be seen racing in the air against one another.

'Rat' racing is particularly suitable for sporting fliers who want to compete against each other without having to bother too much

138 Left — A handy control-line model with a fully-carved balsa body

139 Below — This control-line combat model is made almost entirely from plastic.

140 Right above — A navy carrier flight deck simulated for the operation of control-line models. 1 Take off and free roll area (24 × 8 feet); 2 Arresting lines held by 5 pound sand bags; 3 Island, moved back during operations; 4 Arresting area (20 × 8 feet); 5 Ramp (4 × 8 feet). The control line radius is 60 feet.

141 A control-line model being released from a miniature flight deck

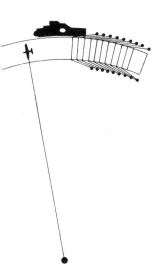

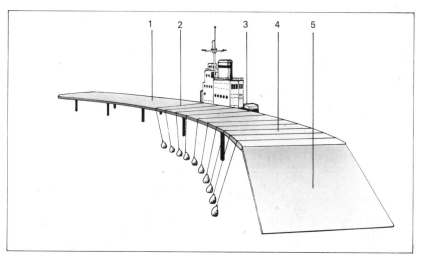

about design specifications. In an event of this kind, two or three models on 60-foot lines are flown continuously for 35, 70 or 140 laps at a time in a series of heat races, stops for re-fuelling being required in the longer heats. A circle of 5-foot radius is laid out on the ground to serve as the outer limit of the pilot's flying base. Outside this, a circle of 15-foot radius limits the pilots' position during take-off, landing and re-fuelling. Pit crews have to remain more than 70 feet from the centre of the circles, and servicing and re-fuelling has to be carried out outside a further circle, of 80-foot radius this time. 'In the event of an accident or entanglement bringing down all planes, a new heat shall be run' is one of the regulations for rat racing enforced by the AMA. A slower and less expensive version of rat racing is provided by control-line 'Good-year' events, in which semi-scale realistic models of actual Good-year racers are flown on lines that are only 52 feet 6 inches long.

The flight standards in contests for flying scale models are covered in the AMA's regulations by a number of precisely expressed definitions. To take – for example – a flying scale-model's take-off:

A Sloppy Take-off is judged when the model is out of control or wobbles and bounces into the air.

A Rough Take-off is judged when the model is instantly air-borne and climbs too steeply with little control, or when the model leaves the ground and then touches the wheels to the ground with a bounce.

A Smooth Take-off is judged when the take-off is under full control, smooth and stable at all times, with the climb resembling that of a full scale airplane.

Control-line combat contests always attract large crowds of admiring spectators. In these contests, each competing model plane draws a crêpe paper streamer behind it. The streamer – in two colours, so that it shall be seen easily – is attached to the plane, and separated from it, by a piece of string of a specified length and strength. The aim of each contestant is to remove, by the skilful manipulation of his plane, all or part of his opponent's streamer without (as the AMA's regulations put it) 'tripping or holding onto his opponent or other unsportsmanlike conduct'. Flights start on a signal from the judges and are of five minutes' duration, or until a 'kill' is made.

'Navy carrier' control line events are especially popular in the United States. In these, semi-realistic models have to simulate the operations carried out by full-scale carrier planes. After flying a high speed phase, each model has to perform a low speed run and then an arrested landing on a scaled-down replica of a naval aircraft carrier deck.

Cox control-line models: above, a Junkers Ju 87D and below, a Douglas *Skyraider*

A line-controlled model performing aerobatics can be an impressive sight, the manoeuvres called for in national and international contests including such spectacular feats as: reverse wing overs, consecutive square loops, hourglass figures, overhead figure eights, and four-leaf clovers. Few control line operators have expressed more graphically their pleasure in their sport than has Vern Clements, of Caldwell, Idaho, who has enjoyed many hours of fully-controlled over-water flying with his *Sure-Fun* seaplane:

'Flying over water, with the model inverted, throttle speed is reduced until stalling-speed is attained; slight down handle control is held, with altitude being controlled by throttle-finger action alone; several practice laps are then flown at this low inverted-flight speed, and 'exhaust music' is played with the throttle finger to develop a keen 'throttle-feel'. Then, using only the throttle finger for altitude control, the rudder is allowed to touch the water during this stalled inverted flight condition; as soon as the rudder sends up a spray of water the throttle finger is pulled back for full power, and this, in conjunction with the 'down' handle control, brings the *Sure-Fun* up and away from the water! This manoeuvre proves the dependability and instant throttle response that is always available when needed. Have heard that spectators turn pale, too, but the flyer is too busy to notice! . . .'

With operations as exact as that to be performed, it is important that great care is given to the selection of the control line. Usually, fish line or some synthetic material such as dacron is used for controlling small models; steel wire, which is heavier, is generally used for controlling larger and higher-powered models. The length of line used depends on the size of the model and the extent of the ground available for it to fly over. If the lines are too long, the control exercised on the plane may not be adequate. If the lines are too short, the model may travel round the operator too quickly, giving the 'man in the middle' no chance to do very much but let it fly rather monotonously in an exactly circular path.

When control-line models are entered for officially sponsored contests, the wires used have to conform to strict specifications. In the rules governing the International Speed Model Class contests held under the auspices of the FAI, for instance, it is stipulated – at the time of going to press – that the distance between the centre of the control handle and the centre line of the model shall be 15·92 metres (52 feet 2¾ inches), and that the thickness of each line shall be not less than 0·3 millimetres (about 0·012 inch). As a safety precaution, models entered in public competitions are usually required to undergo 'pull tests' before they are allowed to

fly. ('The entire control mechanism, from the handle to and including the model, shall be strong enough to withstand a pull test equal to 32 times the weight of the model' is a typical regulation.) These rigorous tests are meant to ensure that the control systems are sufficiently strongly installed so that they do not part company under the stress of high speed flight. In addition, a safety thong connecting the control handle to the pilot's wrist and strong enough to prevent accidental release of the model has usually to be worn.

Even if the greatest care is taken in carrying out the prescribed safety tests, unforeseen circumstances may introduce an element of danger into control-line flying. At the American National Model Airplane Championships held at the Glenview Naval Air Station, Illinois, in 1971, for instance, stiff breezes added an extra hazard, and claimed one notable victim – a beautiful big model of a Boeing B-29 which, after completing many splendid laps, tore loose from its control line and flew off into the distance. The wind,

142 The Beechcraft *Staggerwing*: a simple all-balsa sheet profile control-line model designed by Mike Stott, World Championship Scale Team flier

143 Right – Five spectacular control-line manoeuvres, from top to bottom: reverse wing over, square loop, hourglass figure, overhead figure eight, and four-leaf clover

144 Far right – The beautiful control-line 'Silver' *Hurricane* model marketed by KeilKraft

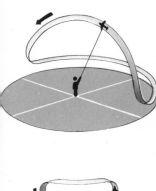

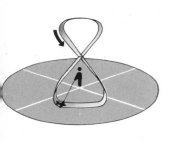

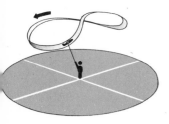

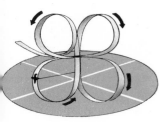

it seems probable, had added enough extra load to open a snap link that had withstood a pull test of over 100 lb only a few moments before. Fortunately, the flyaway model landed in a small clearing. It was a total loss, but none of the spectators was hurt.

Making and flying model aircraft should be an entirely pleasant and harmless occupation, but unfortunately a number of fatal accidents have occurred in aeromodelling circles in several parts of the world, and the majority of these have been caused by the injudicious manipulation of control lines. It is always dangerous to fly a tethered model near high tension wires. Even if the plane misses the power lines by a considerable interval, the high voltage current is liable to jump the gap between them and the control wire or wires, finding its way to the earth, catastrophically, through the operator's body. It is better to be safe than sorry. All aeromodellers should have this rule graven on their hearts: NEVER, NEVER FLY A MODEL AIRCRAFT ANYWHERE NEAR ELECTRICITY LINES!

10 Radio-controlled Model Aircraft

The very first issue of *Model Aviation*, which appeared in June 1936, announced that at the American National Contests to be held shortly after, 'a new contest has been arranged for radio-controlled models'. This stimulated much excitement among the competitors, who were all eager to see a gasoline-powered model fly under radio control. They were to be disappointed, however, for as the editor of *Model Aviation* reported in the second issue, 'Next year we hope to see those radio-controlled ships that failed to show up this year!'.

In 1937, six models were actually entered for the radio control event at the Nationals, and appeared at the meeting. The models were checked in advance by the contest judge who wanted to make sure, while they were still on the ground, that the controls would answer to radio signals. First place was awarded to Chester Lanzo, of Cleveland, Ohio. Lanzo's plane, launched by hand, flew into a nearby parking lot, and although the flight was in a reasonably straight line, the judge and timer noted that every time Lanzo activated the control, the plane could be clearly seen to wobble. Radio control, then, was plainly going to stay.

Keen operators in the new field of research had a slight setback in the 1938 American Nationals, when, on a very windy day, only one radio-controlled plane managed to make a ROG take-off, and that model, after climbing steeply, stalled and crashed after a dive. Doubters were confounded in the following year, though, when a plane built and operated by the twins Walt and Bill Good made a successful flight over a rectangular course that included 'figure-of-eight' turns, and finished at the feet of the controller.

Shortly after Frank Knowles, of Guelph, Ontario, won the Scale Championship at the 1970 Canadian National Radio Control Model Aircraft Contests, he recalled how he was first introduced, a little more than twenty years before, to the hobby at which he had since been so outstandingly successful:

'. . . In 1949 I attended the British Nationals at Fairlop aer[o]-drome which was just outside of London. Other hairless Limeys will probably remember this airfield with its long runways, dozens of football pitches, hundreds of speeding motorcycles and control line and free flight models everywhere. This 1949 Nats. was a well organized competition from the spectators' point of view with all of the flying taking place in one huge roped off arena. I was interested primarily in U-control at that time and so spent my time at the end of the field where the Gold trophy stunt contest was being flown. (Shades of the past – I believe that there were 110 entries in that event that year!) On one side of the arena there was a large crowd clustered around some rather bulky models and everyone told me, with a look of awe on their faces, that this was the radio control competition. I'm afraid that the activity was rather limited but while watching the control line flying I suddenly noticed a huge model airplane of about 12-foot span emerge from the crowd and start to roll down the runway. This machine was most impressive as far as size and seemed to be sporting a large spark ignition motor up front. It unstuck and climbed beautifully if somewhat slowly into the sky and went into a left hand turn. I had heard stories about these aeroplanes with radio control but here before my very eyes was an aeroplane which had raised itself from the ground under its own power and actually made a turn under control. From that moment I was more or less hooked and with the optimism so typical of modellers completely ignored the fact that after making that beautiful turn the model just carried

146 The radio-controlled stunt flier *Triton* marketed by Dumas Products

on flying on its own and disappeared over the far horizon . . .'

It is easy to see, now, why the early radio-controlled flying models had to be large, rather than small. Radio valves and vacuum tubes had not yet been superseded by tiny transistors; room had to be found for 'quench coils' made by winding miles of fine wire round big cylindrical formers, and heavy batteries had to be carried to operate the necessary rubber-band-powered escapements. It was not unusual for a model to be required to fly with a total battery weight of 24 ounces on board.

It is easy to see, too, why the hefty model that so inspired Frank Knowles refused to stay within view for any appreciable length of time. 'Jumbo', as this model seems to have been appropriately called, must have contained gear that would be regarded, today, as relatively primitive.

In principle, the equipment needed to control a model aircraft by radio has not altered much in the intervening years. Now, as then, the operator needs a transmitter to send out his signals; a receiver, in the model, that will intercept these signals; and, also in the model, some device, operated by the receiver, that will move the model's controls according to the instructions given by the operator on the ground. As a result of the enormous advances made in electronic technology in the past two decades, each of these principal components used for the radio control of flying models has been altered and refined almost out of recognition.

47 A pre-World War II American radio-controlled model

1 2 3 4   5   6 7 8   9 10 11

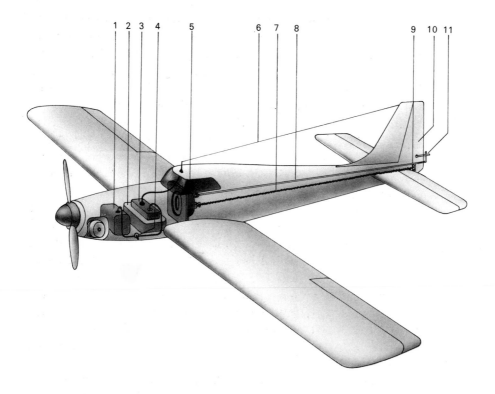

1 2 3   4 5 6   7   8 9   10 11 12   13

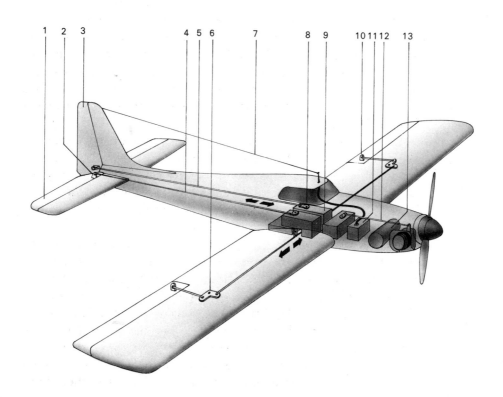

At the time when Frank Knowles was so impressed by the ponderous 'Jumbo', model-makers seeking commercially made radio-controlled equipment would usually be offered gear of the 'carrier-wave' type. In this system, it was only necessary to switch the transmitter on, to get a response from the control mechanism. With an elementary outfit of this kind, the operator would be required to press and release a key on the transmitter to move the rudder of the model from the neutral position to either left or right. Then, he would have to press and release the key again to return the rudder to neutral, and so on, making separate depressions of the key for each move in a simple cycle.

With more complicated carrier-wave outfits, such as the one manufactured at that time by Mercury Cossor, signals could be used to control the elevators, rudder and motor of a model. To transmit the number of pulses needed to move any particular part of the plane, the operator simply had to move a knob on the transmitter to a predetermined position. A spring-driven device in the model that looked like the works of an old alarm clock would then react promptly and correctly to the pulses of the signal – provided, that is, the operator had remembered to wind up the device before the plane left the ground.

The carrier-wave system was soon largely superseded by the tone system. In this, the transmitter is switched on and the radio-frequency signal is transmitted steadily without any reaction being expected from the controls in the model. (This helps to keep the receiver in a state in which it will ignore all but the most powerful forms of interference.) To bring about such a reaction, one or more tones, or musical notes, have to be transmitted to cause a response in the receiver. If more than one tone is sent out, the receiver will separate them and direct them to the units that actually operate the controls in the model.

A receiver used in a tone system will fall into one of two principal categories – it may be 'super-regenerative', in which case it is likely to be relatively small, light, simple and comparatively inexpensive; or it may be 'superheterodyne', in which case it will not be cheap. 'Regens', as experienced radio-control operators usually call receivers of the former type, are very sensitive and they are satisfactorily resistant to interference generated inside the plane that is carrying them, but they are apt to tune broadly and are liable to be affected by any other transmitter that may happen to be operating in the same area on the same megacycle (or 'megahertz') band. So, models fitted with 'Regens' are of little or no use on crowded flying fields. 'Superhets', on the other hand, are selective enough to reject all signals but those they are actually required to receive. It is quite a common sight today to see a varied selection of radio-controlled models flying together above

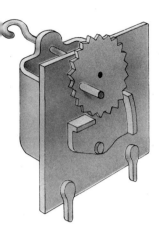

8 Above – A typical single-channel radio installation: 1 battery; 2 shock-proof mounting; receiver; 4 switch; 5 escapement (detail above); 6 aerial; rubber motor to drive escapement; 8 torque rod; winding hook; 10 rudder; 11 rudder-turning mechanism

9 A typical multi-channel radio installation: 1 elevator; 2 elevator horn; 3 rudder; 4, 5 pushrods; 6 aileron crank; 7 aerial; 8 servo bank; 9 servos; 10 aileron horn; receiver; 12 throttle link; battery

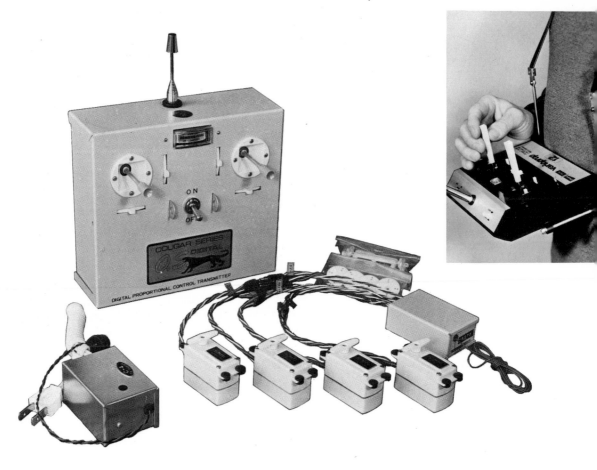

the same field, thanks to the development of the more sophisticated receivers.

Becoming increasingly popular, at the present time, are the control systems classified under the term 'Proportional'. At its simplest, a proportional system involves the sending of a steady series of tone pulses from a transmitter to a receiver in a model. These pulses go out continuously – there may be as many as twenty every second – even when the operator does not wish to alter the position of any control. By altering the relationship between the duration of the 'on' and 'off' periods of the pulse – there will normally be a short control stick on one face of his transmitter for this purpose – the operator is able to change the position of the rudder of his model (or the elevator, or whatever part he wishes to move) to whatever degree he thinks fit, and not merely into a state of full deflection. This gives a much smoother form of control, which is admirably suited for 'stunt' flying and other more advanced manoeuvres.

Radio-control experts attending the American National Model Airplane Championships at the Olathe Naval Air Station, Kansas,

150 Above left – Typical multi-channel radio control equipment

151 Above – Suspension of a transmitter permits unhampered access to, and operation of, all control sticks and knobs

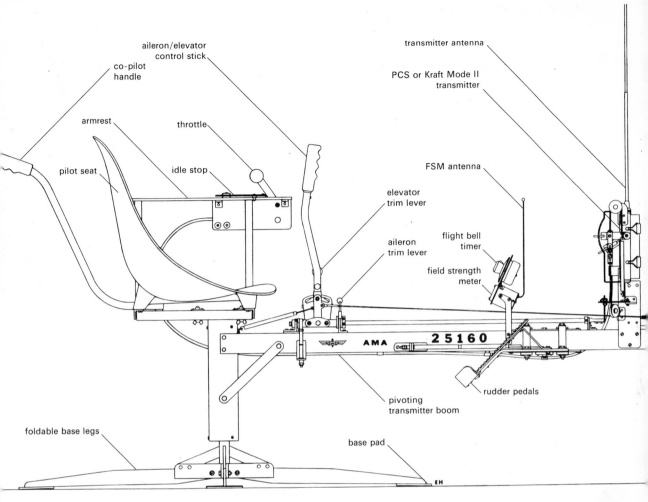

aileron/elevator
control stick

co-pilot
handle

armrest

throttle

pilot seat

idle stop

transmitter antenna

PCS or Kraft Mode II
transmitter

FSM antenna

elevator
trim lever

aileron
trim lever

flight bell
timer

field strength
meter

AMA 25160

foldable base legs

rudder pedals

pivoting
transmitter boom

base pad

52 Diagram of the Fly Seat
invented by Ed Henry

in 1968 were surprised to see a novel exhibit – a 'Fly Seat' made to resemble as nearly as possible the pilot seat of a full-sized airplane. Near the seat were a number of full-scale cockpit controls – again, like those in a real-life prototype. These controls, which included rudder pedals, an aileron/elevator control stick, and a throttle, were linked by a system of cables, pulleys and yokes to a radio control transmitter attached to the end of a pivotting boom. The seat – the brain-child, originally, of Ed Henry of the McDonnell Douglas Radio Control Model Airplane Club, St. Louis, Missouri – had been devised to allow a pilot comfortably settled in it to feel exactly as if he were flying a full scale airplane while he was, in fact, merely flying a lively model. By turning the seat, he could keep the model under continuous visual observation. Cameramen quickly swarmed round this ingenious piece of equipment, and after their photographs of it had been reproduced in various magazines, enquiries for construction plans were received from many different parts of the world. Since then Ed Henry, the designer of the seat – has been prepared, for a small fee, to provide complete information and drawings with all necessary dimensions.

173

Competitions involving radio-controlled model airplanes are regulated carefully by the FAI, the AMA, and other authoritative bodies. In nearly all cases, radio-controlled models flying in official competitions have to conform to certain limitations of weight and engine displacement. Competitors in what are known as 'pattern events' are given this as their objective:

'To control by radio a model airplane so that various planned maneuvers may be accomplished. The criterion is the quality of performance, not the mechanism of control. R/C competition shall be based on the excellence of performance of the model's

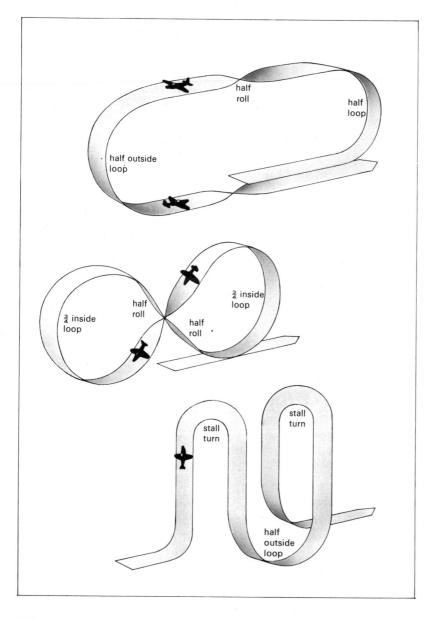

153 Three planned manoeuvres carried out by radio-controlled model aircraft; top to bottom: Double Immelman, Cuban Eight, Figure M

maneuvers compared to similar maneuvers performed by a full size plane . . .'

The list of planned manoeuvres that have to be executed in a given time (usually, eight or ten minutes) is intended to separate skilled operators from the less skilled with a minimum of doubt or ambiguity. Every operator is required to call out to the judges the name of each of his manoeuvres before he attempts to perform it. At the end of the manoeuvre, he has to announce 'manoeuvre complete'. A straight and level exit from a manoeuvre often indicates to a keen judge's eye that a model has tracked well through the course it was intended to take. A typical pattern will include such manoeuvres as these, included (with others equally daunting) in the current FAI World Championship regulations:

FIGURE M: The model starts in straight and level flight, pulls up to a vertical attitude, performs a stall turn (left or right) through 180°, then makes half an inverted loop pulling up again to vertical flight, performs a second stall turn in a direction opposite to the first stall turn and then recovers on the same altitude and heading as the entry. When viewed from the side, the model creates the letter 'M'.

DOUBLE IMMELMAN: The model starts in level flight, pulls up into a half loop, followed by half a roll, flies straight and level for approximately one second, then makes half an outside loop, followed by half a roll, recovering in straight level flight.

CUBAN EIGHT-SAVOY KNOT: The plane commences flying straight and level, pulls up into an inside loop and continues heading downward at 45°, does half roll followed by another inside loop at 45°, does half roll followed by straight and level recovery at same altitude of entry.

All these movements will be watched by critical eyes. A competitor whose plane executes the last of these manoeuvres, for instance, is liable to be down-graded for any of these prescribed reasons:

1. Entry not level
2. Loop not round
3. Loop deviates left or right
4. Roll not on 45° line
5. Second loop not same diameter as first loop
6. Second loop deviates left or right
7. Second loop not at same altitude as first loop
8. Second roll not on 45° line
9. Does not finish level

10. Does not finish on same heading as entry
11. Does not finish at same altitude as entry

Radio-control pylon races are now very popular. The objective is (according to the AMA's regulation book):

'To run multiple plane races that will recapture the spirit and thrills of the great air races of the past and present, and that will be interesting for spectators as well as challenging for the contestants.'

154 Layout of a pylon race course

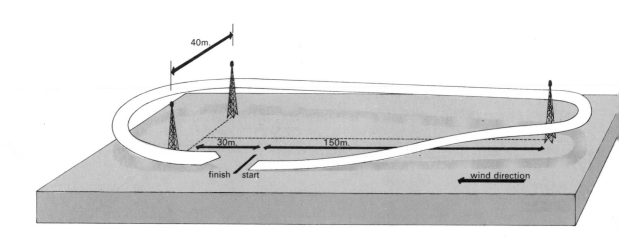

40m.

30m.   150m.

finish start

wind direction

In these races, the models fly round a triangular course marked out, at the corners, by pylons. (Models flying a course of ten laps, with an individual lap length of $\frac{1}{4}$ mile, will have travelled, by the end of the race, 13,200 feet.) Various officials are needed to see fair play in these exciting contests. Marker judges, to check that all the turns at the pylons are legal, are essential, and, in solo races, in which one plane at a time is required to race 'against the clock', a time-keeper who additionally acts as a lap counter is also needed. Quite large sums of money have been known to change hands after the end of radio control pylon races, as they provide convenient opportunities for betting.

Not all competition with radio-controlled model planes is as fierce as this, though. Typical of the many more sociable gatherings that can be enjoyed by well-equipped and competent radio control experts was the Open Scale Contest held by the Ottawa Radio Control Club on 23rd May 1970. On a bright, clear, sunny day, with temperatures near 70°F, thirteen contestants assembled in excellent fellowship, most of them bringing models based accu-

156 Right – A Graupner sailplane converted to powered flying with radio control equipment installed

157 Far right – A KeilKraft *Super Sixty* radio-controlled model

A Schweizer SGS 1—34
plane under radio control

rately on prototypes of World War 2. Late in the afternoon, after preliminary flights and static inspection, these World War 2 models were required to fly on the kind of missions that would have been expected of the real aircraft during their wartime service. The model fighters, for example, carried out various evasive manoeuvres as if they were being pursued by enemy aircraft, gave low-pass support to imaginary forces on the ground, and finished with victory rolls. The model training aircraft performed the kind of exercises that would have been carried out by novice pilots of the 1939–45 period, one operator – Bob Mercer, of Montreal, with a Stearman – providing a real treat for the spectators when he simulated the actions of a not-so-competent tyro out on his first solo. Mercer deliberately almost stalled his aircraft on take off, carried out some spectacularly shaky manoeuvres, and brought the model down to an extremely rough landing – to the sound of delighted applause!

An unusual degree of realism was provided in the team combat contest held later the same evening. In this event, Bob Forest, of Montreal, flying a model of a Fokker Wolfe, went after a model of an Me 109B, flown by Ken Mackenzie, of the Ottawa Club. To add spice to the situation, Mackenzie's Messerschmidt was supposed to be that flown by Hitler's deputy, Rudolf Hess, on his sensational escape from Germany to Scotland. Forest, as the German's top ace, was determined to shoot 'Hess' down before he could reach asylum on the other side of the North Sea. The combat flight was proceeding nicely according to plan when suddenly, while they were 'over England', both pilots sighted the 'inefficient novice' Bob Mercer, flying his Stearman on a training exercise. Naturally, the 'Germans' decided to go after Mercer and shoot him down. Good little guys must always come off best, though, and Mercer, with some quick and violent manoeuvres, managed to evade his ruthless enemies. He landed safely, and the 'Germans' were left to their doom.

In case that happy account should leave a misleading impression, it has to be recorded that skies, in the radio-controlled aeromodel world, have not always been so cloudless, nor have the participants in all radio control competitions been so consistently good humoured. One bone of almost endless contention has been the question of frequencies.

Clearly, in every country where there are aeromodellers using radio control, the limits of the wavebands they may use have to be precisely and firmly defined. In the United States, in 1949, the Federal Communications Commission authorized the use of 465 megahertz for model control and declared that those operating at this frequency would not need to obtain an amateur licence. In 1950, after an impressive amount of research, the General Post

Above, Ed Henry's Fly Seat in front of a radio-controlled model plane

Below, a radio-controlled model at the Manned Spacecraft Center Houston, Texas

Overleaf, a close-up of Dave Platt's radio-controlled super-scale model of a Douglas *Dauntle*

Office in Britain allotted the 27 megahertz spot for the same purpose, and soon, in America, the band between 26·97 megahertz and 27·27 megahertz was made over, with very few restrictions, to the aeromodelling fraternity, the regular frequencies of 26·995, 27·045, 27·095, 27·145, 27·195 and 27·255 megahertz being used by many unlicensed transmitters.

By 1963, however, many American modellers using their so-called 'Citizens' Band' were suffering from intolerable interference from telephone equipment, and the Academy of Model Aeronautics had to raise funds, by inviting public subscriptions, and by soliciting donations from the growing radio control industry, to pay for the services of attorneys who would promote effectively, before the Federal Communications Commission, the interests of their members and other inconvenienced model operators. Funds poured in, and the resulting legal representation paid off handsomely. By June 1966, it had been established that certain new radio frequencies – 72·08, 72·24, 72·96 and 75·64 megahertz – would be reserved by the Commission exclusively for the use of modellers. These frequencies would be incorporated into the existing 'Citizens' Band', too, so that no new licences would be required.

The problem of air space, or the lack of it, is one of the most pressing of all, as, in built-up areas, it is usually difficult, if not impossible, to find places where radio-controlled models can be flown without endangering members of the general public. A disused airport, one might think, would be ideal. One such in the United States attracted numerous radio control enthusiasts who were allowed free use of the place. Then, one disastrous day, a show-off modeller tried flying his little aircraft in formation with a full-size plane landing at a busy airport nearby. Flying of models on the obselete strip was subsequently prohibited. The fliers who had been using the site, dislodged by one of their number's impulsive foolishness, tried to join other clubs in the locality in order to have access to a flying site. Most of these clubs were at capacity membership, as far as the practical use of their fields was concerned, so the frustrated applicants had to turn back to models intended primarily for display!

Preceding page, radio-controlled models of two World War I German fighters: above, the Fokker E. III and below, the Fokker D. VII

Above, an 8-foot span radio-controlled stick model

Below, an all-metal radio-controlled model of the Beagle Pup

11 Free-flight Models

The officers of the FAI define free flight as 'a flight during which there is no physical connection between the aeromodel and the competitor' – recognizing thereby that the vast majority of free flighters are in fact competitive. The book of regulations issued by the officials of the AMA suggests that a free flight model airplane is one which is 'flown without controlling or guide line'. Both definitions are perfectly valid, as one would expect, but, understandably, neither attempts to suggest the appeal that a free-flying aircraft may have for the aeromodeller with a yearning for adventure, and romance.

In many different countries, clubs and associations intended to further the interests of free-flight enthusiasts have been formed. In the United States, for instance, the National Free Flight Society (NFFS) was organized in the early 1960s because many American modellers felt at that time that undue emphasis was being placed, in the national magazines, on radio-controlled models and, to a lesser extent, on control-line flying. The officers of the society quickly recognized that while many thousands of wind-up free-flight models were being assembled from prefabricated kits every year and flown in a hit-or-miss kind of way, the vast majority of those responsible were merely indulging a transitory whim. The more expert free-flight modellers whose interest was likely to be more permanent were being neglected, they found. So, they set out to cater especially for those more serious fliers, their aims being to preserve, enhance and promote the sport and hobby of free-flight model aviation and to act as a unifying body for devoted free flighters. Soon, they were helping the members of the AMA (to which they became affiliated) to make certain much-needed rule changes, and they started to bring out a regular supply of helpful literature. And, they began to work in the closest association with similar free-flight organizations in other parts of the world.

Once a year now, a selection committee appointed by the NFFS chooses a list of the 'top ten' models. The committee's selections in a typical year will include rubber-powered planes, engine-powered models, and hand-launched gliders. In 1971, the top ten

8 Walter Prey's *Drag-Gon*, a free-flight gas model lavishly decorated with pin-striping and tissue cut outs

159 Left – This gas-powered
free-flight model, *Vulcan*, has an
8-foot wing span. It was built in
1952 from a pre-World War II
design.

160 Left below – Sal Taibi holds
Pacer which he designed in
1941 and now flies in 'Oldtimer'
contests

161 Right above – An outstanding
free-flight gas-powered flying
scale model. Harold Warner's
model of the WACO YK56 has
doors that open, complete interior
with seats, instrument panel, map
pocket with maps.

162 Right – Frank Heeb's
Unlimited Rubber *Strato Lark* has
won many important awards

had a nice international mix, models from Canada, Czechoslovakia, England and France being included in the list with those from the United States. All the models chosen were thoroughly practical planes that had won important awards by their excellent performances. Full-sized plans of most of the successful top ten models are normally made available through the society. The willingness of so many designers to co-operate indicates what a good-hearted group of sportsmen have chosen to work in this particular field.

Free-flight model aircraft can be roughly divided into three general categories, regardless of the way in which they are powered.

First, there are the flying scale models intended to resemble, to the highest possible degree, a full-size prototype. Fulton Hungerford's Ford Trimotor described in Chapter 6 is a splendid example, but free-flight models as fine as this are rare.

The second category of free-flight models includes all those designed and built for the personal enjoyment of the modeller, rather than for scale quality or competitive flying. Sporting models of this kind, having no need to be particularly realistic or particularly efficient, can afford to be relatively heavy and their engines – if they have engines – do not have to be particularly powerful.

In the third category we find all the free-flight models made with the specific purpose of contest-winning.

When free-flight contests first started, modellers could enter any kind of plane, powered with any kind of engine, and carrying as much fuel as the plane was capable of lifting. When an increasing number of models flew away out of sight and were lost for ever (or were returned, perhaps in pieces in paper bags, like the errant aircraft belonging to one unfortunate operator which, he was told, had been run over by a train) some form of limitation on performance was obviously called for. So, rules were formulated by which the fuel carried by a competing plane was not allowed to exceed more than $\frac{1}{4}$ ounce for each pound of the plane's weight. Still, valuable planes continued to fly away into the almost infinite distance, and soon a further edict had to be laid down – that engines should only be allowed to run for thirty seconds. This limitation had to be further reduced when the loss-rate continued to soar. At the time of writing, free-flight contest models in the United States are permitted an engine run of twelve seconds only, and even that could have been reduced by the time this book appears.

Free-flight contest models have to be designed, then, in such a way that they will climb as high as possible in as short a time as possible, and then glide to earth in a gentle and thoroughly reliable way. (Finding thermal currents on which a model can ride is a recognized refinement of the successful free-flight

63 Bruce Hannah's shirt matches his *Classic Elite* model. Checkerboard tissue can be bought at most hobby shops

operator's techniques.) Clearly, a model that has to perform two entirely different functions – to climb steeply like a powerfully-engined interceptor fighter and then to glide slowly down like a motorless sailplane – must be designed in such a way that the best possible results can be obtained during each different stage of the plane's journey. To achieve this, it will obviously be desirable at some point to change the shape of the model's wing or wings, since an airfoil with little or no camber, suitable for speed, is quite different from a gliding airfoil which has to be highly arched so as to provide high lift values. If a model having a wing with a lot of camber and, therefore, lift is sent skywards in a modern, near-vertical climb, the wing with its unwanted curvature is liable to

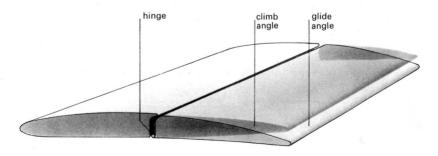

64 A typical wing section of a 'flapper'

pull the airplane off pattern into a loop that is likely to prove disastrous.

So, 'flappers' have been developed – wings fitted with hinged flaps to give variable airfoil sections. Ideally, aboard planes with such wings, there should be a finger-sized pilot who will alter its trim to suit each particular phase of the flight. As this is quite impossible, real-life midgets as small as this being in extremely short supply, appliances activated by non-human sources of power have had to be devized.

Shortly after World War 2, some bright European aeromodellers were a little disconcerted by the unprecedented power developed by the newly-introduced miniature diesel engines. Their planes, driven by these units, were all too liable to shoot off pattern into wild loops, or to turn away into disastrous spiral dives. So, they developed devices to control these regrettable tendencies.

First of the innovators to be really successful was the Belgian, Gaston Joostens, who invented an ingenious pendulum-powered monitor to be fitted at the rear end of each of his diesel-powered model planes. By using a swinging weight, Joostens ensured that as long as the model was climbing steeply its rudder would remain straight. If the machine started to turn to the right or left, the rudder would be moved automatically the other way, and the plane's deviation would be immediately corrected. When a Joostens model stopped climbing and started to glide down to earth, the rudder would react less readily to the pressures imposed on it by the pendulum. The way Joostens arranged the hinges saw to that.

Joosten's ideas immediately caught the attention of other modellers, and soon several of his associates were experimenting successfully with pendulum-powered monitors that would control (besides the rudders of their planes) the elevators or the ailerons, or, by a bit of really tricky contrivance, the elevators *and* the ailerons. One famous model of a Percival *Mew Gull* – designed and constructed by a P. E. Norman – was able to travel with exemplary steadiness at speeds above 50 m.p.h. because it was under the unerring influence of the movable weight-operated elevators Norman had designed for it. Other models built by Norman were able to perform prolonged programmes of advanced aerobatics without plunging to destruction. These lively little planes were corrected, whenever they strayed off the paths planned for them, by some of the most subtle and efficient pendulum-controlled systems that have ever been devized. After that, the 'gadget kings' moved in. Now, many free-flight contest models have propellers that will fold up and tuck their blades back out of the way at some pre-ordained instant in time, and variable-pitch propellers are comparatively common.

5 Richard Mathis launches, at
1972 United States National
ntests, a free-flight model he
signed in collaboration with
m Peadon

Nowadays, too, every free-flight model aircraft that is liable to vanish for ever over the horizon is likely to be fitted with a 'dethermalizer' – a device that will function after a pre-determined interval of time, causing the model to descend as swiftly and safely as possible to earth. In most instances, the model is allowed to fly freely for five minutes, which is the duration permitted by the rules of most contests, and is known familiarly as a 'max'. Only in fly-offs are longer flight times than this likely to be called for.

Dethermalizers – the successful ones – fall into two principal categories.

Most reliable of all are the spring-loaded dethermalizers that will alter the trim of the stabilizers or horizontal tails of the models to which they are fitted so that the noses of the models will be raised suddenly, causing them to stall. It it is nicely adjusted, a model fitted with a dethermalizer of this kind will descend rapidly to the ground with its nose held considerably higher than its tail. Several clockwork devices are sold that will operate, after the required interval of time, a dethermalizer of this type. Alternatively, a slow-burning fuse (made, generally, of string soaked in strong saltpetre) may be used, but a timer of this kind has to be effectively

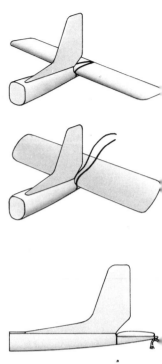

insulated or it may set fire to the model it is meant to preserve. Even more disastrously, it may start a forest fire. In many areas, the authorities insist that any fuse carried in a model aircraft shall be safely contained in a metal snuffer tube.

Only a little less popular is the dethermalizer which does its job by releasing, at the required moment, a parachute that acts as a brake on the plane by slowing its glide. A device of this kind may be operated by either a mechanical timer or a fuse.

However carefully it may be protected against the vagaries of unforeseeable thermal currents that may lift it up at one moment into the empyrean and, at the next, may let it fall disappointingly to the ground, with however much cunning it may be guarded against unpredictable breezes that will try to divert it to left or right as it flies some hundreds of feet above the earth's surface, the free-flight model is, in the whole world of model aircraft, one of the very worst security risks. Clearly, free flight would be an impossibly uneconomic activity if there were no means at all of finding a phenomenally successful model plane once it has vanished, apparently for ever, over the horizon. Fortunately, as the sophistication and cost of free-flight model aircraft have in-

6 Left above – Diagramatic ~ws of a fuse-operated ~hermaliser, before and after ~ease

7 Left below – Elton Drew's ~rdic A/2 glider, *Lively Lady*, ~n the Swedish Cup at Weiner ~ustadt, Austria in 1969

8 Below – Mike Meuser about ~release his solid balsa catapult ~der. Models of this kind remain ~pular with the Oakland Cloud ~sters, the well-known American ~e-flight group started in 1936.

creased, so too has the interest taken in the problem of recovery.

Under the rules of the FAI, the AMA, and other bodies, radio transmitters may be fitted into free-flight models, though radio control receivers are not allowed. So, in the late 1960s, free-flight exponents started to experiment with small low-powered recovery transmitters that would continue to send out easy-to-pick-up signals after the models in which they were fixed had 'downed'. Then the great firms that were starting to cater for the steadily expanding American model rocket world began to produce and market similar devices on a commercial scale. Soon, many of these

169 Left – Bill Blanchard with one of his famous hand-launched *olly* gliders

170 Marty Thompson's *Forty us* cargo class model carried a oss weight of 20·5 oz and elped him to win a Boeing cholarship in 1972

transmitters were being bought for use in free-flight model aircraft.

The design and production of hand-launched gliders (HLG) is an activity becoming increasingly popular in the free flight world today. 'HLG is where free flight begins', enthused Mark Valerius of Houston, Texas, recently. 'It provides more air time, and fun, per dollar, or hour, invested than any other phase of this marvellous avocation. We cannot over emphasize, to beginners especially, the rewards these lovely little birds have to offer'. To win an outdoor contest with a free-flight glider requires every inch of height the operator can get and every second of glide time descending, Valerius had reasoned. So he had faced the fact that gaining a number of first places would result in a correspondingly large number of lost gliders (he computed the wastage as roughly one ship per 'max'). Once he had fully developed the design of his lively little *Plane Jane*, Valerius assembled a set of simple jigs and tools which would enable him to reproduce, quickly and reliable, more gliders to exactly the same dimensions.

Some of the most successful hand-launched model gliders that have ever been made have been given the light-hearted type name *Polly* by their maker Bill Blanchard, who is a member of the American National Free Flight Society. Blanchard got the idea for his gliders after the 1963 National Championships, but as he was on National Service he was not able to do much constructive work until 1967. As if to compensate for this enforced delay, he managed to build more than fifty different *Pollys* in the next four years, reducing the wing span from 20 inches to 18 inches, for economic reasons, after he had completed approximately a dozen of them.

Foremost of the qualities Blanchard expected of his model gliders is consistency, and many features to achieve the required performance are incorporated in the design. The models' most important structural members – their hefty fuselages – are made from balsa, since Blanchard has found that these have a rigidity not normally associated with fuselages of the ever-popular spruce type of equal weight. Aided by this rigidity, Blanchard has been able to increase the effectiveness of the launching flights of his *Pollys* until the little craft have reached extraordinary altitudes. With such starts, their success in important competitions has been almost inevitable. Three times in one year, Blanchard has managed to raise the record for hand-launched model gliders, finishing with a flight that lasted for 22 minutes.

There is room in the free-flight world for many different types of less orthodox models. For instance, free-flight model helicopters are frequently seen. A model of this kind is defined by the officials of the AMA as 'an aircraft which derives its sustaining lift from rotating airscrew(s) operating in a substantially horizontal

First of the famous Sig
'Classic Series', the *Cabinaire*,
designed by Paul McIlrath,
captures the unforgettable lines of
high wing cabin airplane of the
'30s

plane'. Model helicopters should be capable of vertical take-off
descent and directional flight, the Academy's supplemental and
provisional rules state, and they stipulate – for safety's sake – that
no metal rotors may be used.

There is room in the free-flight world, too, for contests of many
unusual kinds. Popular at the present time are 'Payload' or 'Cargo'
competitions. In these, model aircraft which are flown without
controlling or guide lines have to carry dummy pilots and simulated
freight that has to conform to certain specified size and weight
limits. No mechanical device or added power may be used to
assist a model which is competing in one of these contests to rise
from the ground, though hand-launched flights may occasionally
be permitted where the launching area is unsuitable, through
roughness or any other deficiency, for a normal take-off.

Organized by the NFFS, the United States Free Flight Championships held in October 1971 at Taft, California, saw two
hundred and fifty contestants from nine states – from Arizona,
Colorado, Connecticut, Indiana, Michigan, Oregan, Texas and
Washington, as well as from California itself – and from Canada
and Mexico come together for three action-jammed days (and
nights). Twenty events were flown in perfect weather conditions
in flat treeless desert that extended downwind for ten miles. The

Night Flying Contest – a popular event in the western states of America – attracted eighteen entries. At almost any time during this contest, at least one new 'satellite' could be seen weaving a geometrically perfect light pattern against the background of the starry sky. Next morning, a team of helpers in cars and cycles threaded their way through the sagebrush in search of the few models that had failed to return to home base.

Competition, in the free-flight sphere, between the chosen representatives of the great aeromodelling nations is extremely keen. Thirty-two countries were represented in the FAI's Free Flight World Championships held in Säve, near Gothenburg, Sweden in July 1971, fifty-eight competitors flying gliders, forty-four power-driven planes, and fifty-two rubber-powered aircraft. Light full-sized planes were used for spotting flyaway models, and a large team of recovery men was on hand to bring back quickly the few that got away.

When such important contests are held, involving so many people, it is vitally important that a suitable flying site is found, as trees or rocky terrain may damage models and impede recovery. The site at Säve was particularly open to criticism in this respect. The winner of the Powered Model Championship – Rolf Hagel, of Sweden – was victorious in spite of the fact that the leading edge of his model's wing was broken when the model landed among boulders during the five minute fly-off round. Hagel's pride and joy then had to remain outdoors overnight but managed to remain more or less immune to the potentially disastrous humidity. Hazards like this may add an extra spice of excitement to free flight, but most operators would gladly do without them.

Above, a free-flight model of a Stampe SV4A

Below, a 6-foot span petrol-driven free-flight model, *Pacemaker*, designed in 1941

12 The Commercial World of Model Aircraft

The history of commercially produced model aircraft has been shaped, like most gripping real-life chronicles, by a few dynamic men with larger-than-life-size personalities.

One of the original heroes of the model aircraft trade was Charles Hampson Grant, whose great-grandfather John Hampson designed and supervised the building of the *De Witt Clinton*, the first engine to pull a passenger train on the New York Central Railroad, and whose grandfather, Edward P. Hampson, supplied the lighting machinery for the Statue of Liberty. Charles Grant who, as long ago as 1909, built a single stick pusher model plane that came within ten feet of the 431-foot world record held at that time by Percy Pierce, has been called by many admirers 'The Father of Model Aviation'.

During World War 1, Grant was assigned to the Technical Section of the Air Service at Washington, D.C. While there, he worked, among other projects, on the designs of a new full-sized pursuit plane. In his spare time, such as it was, he developed further models. When he was honourably discharged in 1919, Grant was approached by a group of Dayton businessmen who offered to put reproductions of his models on the market. Soon, the Middle West states were flooded with Grant-blessed model planes that would fly distances that ranged between 100 and 2,000 feet. (Grant, personally, invented a machine by which one man with a single helper could shape 1,000 model airplane propellers in the course of a single working day. At that time, this was a really big deal). The company failed, in 1921, due to poor business conditions, but Grant was undeterred.

Grant's great come-back was made in 1928, when he perfected an exceedingly practical and foolproof model plane. This was so generally covetable that the Grant Aircraft Company, organized specially to reproduce it and to sell the replicas, was unable to supply them fast enough to meet the demand. Soon, Grant had to lease the right to manufacture 'his' models to the Kingsbury Manufacturing Company of Keene, New Hampshire. During the next two years, more than 200,000 aluminium model aircraft were

free-flight model of the S.E.5a

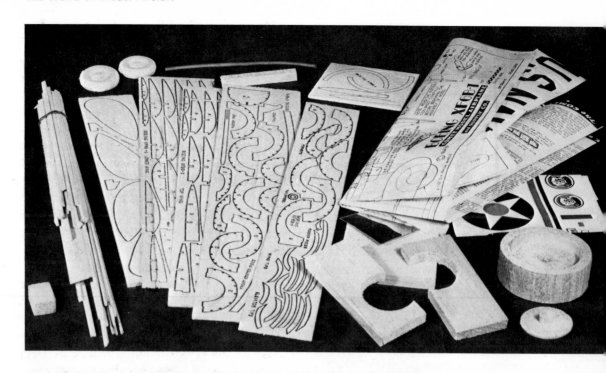

sold by this company. There were six different designs, each of which had been drafted, or at least approved, by Grant, but all were marketed as the *Kingsbury Silver Arrow*.'The great 1929 depression came along then, and sent the previously flourishing model aircraft industry into the steepest of earthbound nose dives.

By the late 'thirties, a measure of recovery had been made. Kits, with clear and detailed instruction sheets, by which 'model aircraft that would really fly' could be constructed with a minimum of supervision by any reasonably handy youngster, were being offered by the hundred in hobby shops in all civilized parts of the world. And, the growth of this great and educationally valuable industry has gone on steadily ever since then. One American manufacturer of stick-and-paper intermediate and advanced kits has estimated recently that he produces 350,000 yearly, or 1,500 per working day. And, he manages to sell them!

The largest manufacturers of model kits in Britain at the present time are E. Keil and Company. This firm was originally situated in Hackney in East London, where its owners had been established for a considerable number of years as furniture manufacturers. In 1938, they started to make model construction kits, and by 1955 the demand for their products was so great that shortage of space compelled them to move out into the country – to Wickford, in Essex. The buildings in which 'Keilkraft' model kits and accessories are manufactured now cover 15,000 square feet, and 120 people are kept fully employed by the company.

Outstanding in the present Keilkraft range of kit-built gliders are the *Magpie* (a model suitable for beginners that is very easy both to build and fly); the rugged and dependable *Gnome*; and the *Marauder*, a contest sail plane intended for the advanced flier, which is capable of a very high standard of performance. In the range of free flight and radio control kits offered by Keilkraft, the accurate scale model of the *Tiger Moth* – one of the most popular aircraft, at one time, in the world – can be guaranteed to take the eye. Keilkraft kits from which most efficient control-line planes can be built include the *Midge* – a speed model that will accommodate 1 cubic centimetre – 1·5 cubic centimetre engines and which was, for a period, the British record holder for planes in that category – and the *Crusader*, an advanced stunt model of superb performance and outstanding looks that has a wingspan of 56 inches. As well as the necessary plans and directions, both for construction and flying, a typical Keilkraft kit may contain die-cut sheets of high grade balsa on which have been printed the shapes of all wing ribs, formers, and other parts; an ample quantity of best strip balsa; a plastic propeller and a plastic spinner or nose plug; plastic wheels; shaped undercarriage legs; wire; covering tissue; sheet celluloid and (if the plane is to fly by rubber power) a suitably tested motor.

72 An early kit from which a model of the Boeing XFGB.1 *Comet* could be made

73 A partly completed model of a Boeing P-12 built from a 1932 'Cleveland' plan

203

The kits in this manufacturer's 'Flying Scale' series contain realistically shaped plastic cockpit covers.

Ripmax Limited – also a British firm – was started in 1949. It is not difficult to see how the company's name was evolved, since the enterprise began as a partnership between Charles Arthur Ripon (better known in the modelling world as 'Rip') and Max Coote, who is still one of the directors. As well as producing and marketing dozens of different kits with which a wide range of flying models can be constructed, Ripmax are notable for having introduced, in 1956, the first fully-sealed radio control receiver (known as the 'Ripmax *Pathfinder* Unit') and for having presented to the British Society of Model Aeronautical Engineers the first trophy for radio-controlled course flying.

From Kirchheim-Teck, in Germany, come the famous Graupner kit models that are on sale in most parts of the world. Graupner offer a number of fully equipped, ready-to-fly models too, and others, like their little *Mini Piper* power model, which take only a couple of hours or so to prepare for flying.

A whole new era in aeromodelling started during World War 2, when the United States' government found that it needed large number of small scale models of aircraft to help with the identification of the many full-sized planes that were hurtling at high speeds

174 A partly constructed model of a Westland *Lysander*. This was produced with a pre-World War II British Keelbild kit.

175 The completed *Lysander* model

176 A Mercury model of Aeronca *Sedan* suitable for free-flight or single-channel radio control

through the world's sadly disturbed skies. Schools, appealed to, could not produce the models quickly enough. So, the powers-that-were had to appoint a plastics manufacturer to mass produce the models for them. Irwin Polk – another energetic and colourful figure who, at that time, was head of the model industry association's war effort committee – negotiated for the sale of these replicas to civilians. Marketed under the evocative name *Aristo-Craft*, these little war-aids introduced plastics most profitably to the American hobby trade and, subsequently, to the model manufacturers of most other civilized countries.

Plastic construction kits – as marketed, today, in enormous numbers – appeal particularly to those people of all but the very youngest age groups, who want to make realistic and reasonably accurate scale models of aircraft, but who lack the skills necessary for making minutely detailed models from scratch or from elaborate kits of the type described in Chapter 6. Assembling the parts provided with a plastic kit and applying a suitable finish is an

7 Model Aircraft (Bournemouth)
d have produced this elegant
3-inch span kit model of a
opwith '1½ Strutter'. This is
itable for 2-channel proportional
dio control

78 Specially prepared for speedy
sembly the Graupner kit of
hich these are the component
arts produces a lively radio-
ntrolled *Consul* model.

79 The completed *Consul* model

instructive exercise, as well as being a thoroughly enjoyable pastime.

Among the foremost producers of plastic kit models in the whole of the world now is the massive United States-based firm of Revell Incorporated. The history of the great Revell enterprise began in the early 1950s, when the founders of the company introduced the world's first scale model car kits, in plastic. Soon, more advanced and highly detailed models were developed, and a number of aircraft were added to the range. From its quite humble beginnings in Venice, California, Revell has grown to occupy a $10\frac{1}{2}$-acre headquarters at which more than 500 people are employed. Revell products are manufactured in several other countries, too, and are sold in more than eighty. In the first twenty-nine years of Revell activity, the company has produced and sold more than 233,000,000 separate units.

Though a Revell kit can be purchased in a hobby shop, a chain, or department store for just a few dollars, the master mould for that model is likely to cost as much as $50,000 and often will cost considerably more. Before the kit can be marketed, executives of the company have to carry out an enormous amount of research and development, planning, engineering, manufacturing, packaging and advertising. To justify all this work, to recover the large sums of money invested in the enterprise, and to show a reasonable profit, the model offered must have exceptional appeal. How, then is the prototype selected?

Probably, a customer will write in to suggest a subject that he considers should be available in kit model form. This proposal will be passed along to the company's Advance Development Department, who evaluate the suggestions and make recommendations to the Revell management. If the management team approves the project, they will forward it to the Revell engineering staff. An engineer will then be specially assigned to the project and given responsibility for designing the model in such a way that it will be economical to manufacture, and practical to assemble.

From the detailed engineering specifications, a hand-built original model must be created by highly skilled craftsmen. From this original model, plaster and epoxy resin moulds are made. These moulds are then used as patterns for the steel tools and dies which are cut on pantograph machines. Finally, the steel dies are finished by hand, fixed in a suitable base, and installed in a powerful injection moulding machine. This machine, handled by a single semi-skilled operator, can turn out in thirty seconds a kit that has been in the research, development and engineering stages for almost a year.

The whole exciting chronicle of man's adventures in the air is unfolded in Revell's authentic aircraft model collection, claim

Above, commercially-made propeller spinners and canopies

Below, a kit model of the radio-controlled model, *Taxi*, with its control apparatus

Overleaf, Maxey Hester's world-famous radio-controlled kit model of the Ryan STA Special

their PR department. The world's most sensational airplanes, from the triplanes that flew in World War 1 to the most modern jet fighters are represented in colourful, fully detailed, precisely engineered models. In Revell's highly popular $\frac{1}{32}$-scale series, for instance, there are model kits of the P-40E *Flying Tiger*, the Hawker *Hurricane* Mark 1, the Grumman F4F-4 *Wildcat*, the Junkers Ju 87B *Stuka*, and many other historic aircraft. The comparatively large size of the models in this series means that there can be lots of moving parts, such as reach-in cockpits with accurate instrument panels, fuselage openings that reveal beautifully detailed model engines, rotating propellers and (in some cases) retractable landing gear. With certain specified Revell kits, certificates are supplied that enable the purchaser to obtain long-play 7-inch records which reproduce the actual sounds made by the machine being modelled.

Another big range of plastic construction kits is offered by Airfix Products – a company based in Britain but selling its wares, like Revell, in many different parts of the world.

Since Airfix models have become so popular, many people have asked how the name came into being. The company was started before World War 2 by Nicholas Koves, and at first its only function was the production of air-filled mattresses. Koves, who was interested in phonetics, had a fondness for words ending with the letters 'IX'. He believed, too, in the value to a company of a name that began with the letter 'A' and would therefore be given a place at the head of all lists and in the opening pages of all trade catalogues. Since his employees 'fixed air' into mattresses, Koves did not take long to decide the name of his company.

When wartime disturbances in Asia cut off virtually all his supplies of rubber, Koves had to turn to other activities. Like many other small manufacturers at that time, he did what he could with the scarce materials available, managing to produce goods that ranged from utility cigarette lighters (made from scrap metal) to saw-cut plastic combs. His success with the latter led him, almost automatically, into being the purchaser of the first British-made injection moulding machine. Soon, Koves had developed a huge business in injection-moulded combs.

In 1948, when the sellers' market in plastic combs had dwindled noticeably, Koves travelled to the United States, and on returning to Britain, crammed with ideas, he decided to move into the plastic toy business. Later in the same year, his company produced its first construction kit – for making a Ferguson farm tractor. The moulding and packaging materials available at that time were not at all satisfactory, however, and it was not until 1952, when the first of the present range of Airfix construction kits was produced and marketed through Woolworths' stores, that the full potential

Two Revell plastic-kit models: above, a Kawasaki *Toryu* and below, a Sopwith *Camel*

213

180 A collection of 1:72 scale plastic kit models seen at an aeromodellers' rally

of the market became apparent. Soon, Airfix plastic construction sets were being sold by the thousand to the many people in Europe who, owing to the difficult post-war circumstances, had insufficient room in their homes for more traditional hobbies.

Each Airfix series, now, contains a number of different but loosely related designs, executed throughout to a consistent scale – usually, 1:72. A modeller exploring the resources of the Airfix Series 4, for example, can build superbly detailed replicas of the German Dornier Do 17 – known, often, as the 'Flying Pencil' – which was first put into service in Spain during the Spanish Civil War, and was afterwards used during World War 2 as a reconnaissance aircraft; the Handley Page *Hampden*, which was operated by the British Royal Air Force during most of the same war as a bomber and, later, for mine laying and torpedo dropping; the McDonnell *Phantom* F-4, an American two-seater, heavy-duty, fighter-bomber that combined abnormally high speeds with the ability to deliver vast loads of armament from both aircraft carrier and airfield; the North American RA-5C *Vigilante*, a development of the twin-jet carrier-based *Vigilante* series, which had the latest

81 A Revell plastic kit model of
Curtis P-40E

reconnaissance equipment carried in a pod beneath the fuselage; the Northrop P 61 *Black Widow*, the first American aircraft to be designed specifically as a night fighter; the Ilyushin Il-28, one of the earliest Russian jet-bombers; the North American B-25 *Mitchell*; and many more. The last mentioned kit contains 120 different pieces, and the working parts provided include movable control surfaces, a rotating gun turret, and opening bomb doors.

Frog International Scale Model Assembly Kits – produced, at the time of going to press, by Rovex Industries of Margate, England – include the original 'Combat Series'. Each kit in this series contains the parts and transfers needed to make two complete models – the Hawker *Hurricane* and the Junkers Ju 87G *Stuka* are paired as worthy opponents, as are the Supermarine *Spitfire* and Junkers Ju 88, and the Bristol *Blenheim* Mark I and the Messer-schmidt Bf 109F. The kits also contain a standing frame in which can be displayed the action picture from the front of the box in which the components are marketed. By attaching the two made-up models to the frame, a very attractive three-dimensional picture can be completed. Revell, in their 'Fighting Deuces' series, match

the Hawker *Hurricane* against the Focke-Wulf Fw-190, and the Supermarine *Spitfire* against the Me 262. Other dogfighting duos of World War 2 recalled by Revell include those between the Mitsubishi *Zero* and the Grumman *Wildcat*, and between the P47 *Thunderbolt* and the Kawaski *Hien*.

Before an absolute beginner starts any kind of plastic kit building, a few inexpensive but necessary tools have to be acquired. A craft or hobby knife with some spare blades will be essential, and one manufacturer recommends the use of a small 'razor' saw. A pair of tweezers will be needed for picking up and holding the smaller components. For cleaning away any unwanted material, a half-round and a round jeweller's file (or 'rat-tail' file) will be useful. For drilling holes in the plastic – for example, to take rigging wires – a small 'pin' drill is advocated by another manufacturer. (No chuck is needed for a drill of this type as it can be rotated between finger and thumb.) A pair of scissors and a small screwdriver – both normally found in the home workshop – will be occasionally called into service.

To be wholly successful, a model-maker who starts with a plastic construction kit has to be both deliberate and patient. When he unpacks the parts he is to assemble, he will find, usually, that they are still joined by the moulding racks or 'sprues' that connected them when they came from the high-pressure injection-moulding machine which gave them their permanent shape. If he is rash, he will cut (or, worse, break) the parts away from the sprues without pausing to consider what he is doing. Later, when he has some

3 An Airfix plastic kit model of
North American *Vigilante*

4 A Frog plastic kit model of a
Junkers Ju 86b

5 A Frog plastic kit model of a
Lockheed *Lightning*

very small component to paint, he may find that his task would have been easier if that component were still attached securely to its sprue.

Inevitably, most of the parts will have to be cleaned before they are assembled. Many will have flashings or mould marks to be filed away or smoothed down with abrasive paper. (Fine glasspaper or 'wet or dry' paper is generally used for plastic models.) Some surface marks that appear on the prototype will have been moulded into the surface of the plastic by the kit manufacturer's pattern makers, but a careful study of photographs and drawings of the full-sized plane should indicate which of the detail marks belong on the model and which have merely resulted from the moulding process. All parts should be carefully checked for fit in case there has been any distortion during the moulding.

For joining the components polystyrene cement is usually supplied. It comes, normally, in tubes and should be used in the smallest possible quantities to make fine films of adhesive between the surfaces to be joined. The cement can be applied to these surfaces with a match stick or tooth pick, trimmed so that it makes a convenient spreader, or with the end of a thick pin. (In the caps of some tubes, applicators will be found that are useful for spreading the cement in tight areas.) Sprung clothes pegs or office clips can be used for clamping small parts together while the cement sets. For holding larger components temporarily together, transparent adhesive tape is useful.

186 Assembling the engine of a Frog plastic model of a Westland *Wapiti,* a two-seater general purpose biplane

Many model-makers are quite satisfied once they have assembled the parts of their plane in this way, but if the model is to look exactly like the real thing, the fact that it is only made of plastic pieces must somehow be effectively disguised. Principal giveaways are the seams left, after assembly, where the individual parts adjoin. For covering these seams and for filling unwanted gaps, special liquid cements can usually be purchased from the retailers who supply the kits, or, alternatively, automobile body putties can be used. When dry, these fillers should be filed and rubbed with abrasive paper until they form part of the model's surfaces.

Many of the parts supplied with plastic kits are pre-coloured in hues and tints that approximate to those found in the real life plane, but not many model-makers are content with these. The addition of some coats of paint, they find, helps to conceal any colour differences that may be emphasizing the seams just described, and also mask the apparent translucency that is common to all plastic kit components, and is most unrealistic.

When all file marks have been smoothed away, the model should be washed thoroughly with soap and water – to remove any traces of grease or lubricant that may have been left on its surfaces when the plastic parts came from the mould, or during assembly – and then rinsed and dried. Care must then be taken to see that the model is not handled again until the recommended grey primer coat and the colours are quite dry.

The colours chosen for a plastic kit model can completely alter its appearance. While some modellers are content to match the colours shown in the picture of the prototype on the box in which the kit has been marketed or, in some cases, in a guide provided with the instruction sheets, other modellers enjoy doing their own research. This may take some time, since the prototype aircraft may have had its livery changed several times during its working existence. There is a wide range of 'decals' or transfer sheets on the market with which the special surface markings of almost any plane popular with modellers can be easily and accurately applied. In most cases, one of these sheets will be included with the kit.

Some people who assemble plastic kit models with pieces exactly as they come from the box tire eventually, of an activity that is so straightforward. But prototype aircraft are anything but standard-

87 An interesting conversion job Frog plastic kit models of a Junkers Ju 88 (at foot) and a Focke-Wulf 190 have been skilfully combined to make this model of a *Mistel* composite aircraft

ized. To take a very notable example – the Messerschmitt Me 262 had fighter, night fighter, bomber, reconnaissance and many experimental versions developed during its short but exciting career. The De Havilland *Mosquito* – another example – had interchangeable components by which it was made, variously, into a bomber, a fighter, a reconnaissance plane and a transport aircraft. And, many a less historic prototype may be, at the end of its trials period, a noticeably different machine from the one that first emerged from the experimental hangar. The creative urges of an energetic kit-modeller may be satisfied more completely if he undertakes a few 'conversion jobs'.

Before he can carry out a successful conversion the modeller may have to do a considerable amount of preliminary research. At first, he will probably decide to undertake a purely superficial conversion, which may involve a certain amount of detail alteration, such as a change of colour scheme, or a change of markings, without calling for any extensive carving up. Later, he will only be satisfied with a conversion that involves changes in a few, at least, of the important features of the kit-provided model. The propeller, in the new version, may have to have three blades instead of two; the nose contours may have to be altered by being filed and sanded to suit the new propeller boss; and the exhaust may have to have open ports instead of manifolds. Changes in the prototype may have been made in fairly rapid succession. When this has been the case, it is essential that the modeller who wishes to be historically accurate should represent the exact design at one particular stage in the development of the type.

The departure of the American astronauts for the moon and their travels on its surface opened up some new vistas in the world of commercial model 'aircraft'. Revell now market a number of fine kits that have been directly inspired by the almost incredible achievements of twentieth century man. In faithful detail, the models produced from these kits depict the spacemen as well as their craft, and manage to suggest the high adventure of a few of the more spectacular missions. Revell's kit model of the Apollo/Saturn V Moon Rocket System, made to 1:96 scale, is nearly four feet high when complete. Beautifully engineered, and of compulsive interest to the space-minded, is the model, made to 1:48 scale, of the Lunar Module shown as if it is at rest at Tranquillity Base. (Gold foil covering, matching that on the real life vehicle, is provided with this kit.) Airfix, too offer an exciting range of 'space age' kits, among their very popular subjects being the SH-3D *Seaking* – the famous helicopter 'Sixty-Six' used to recover the astronauts from the ocean after each Apollo mission. When complete, this model shows an astronaut being winched on board the helicopter.

Model rocket at lift-off. Thirty-six of these *Patriots* opened the Transpo 72 Airshow, the entire group firing in about 12 seconds

13 Model Rocketry

On the 16th March 1926, at Auburn, Massachusetts, a Robert H. Goddard launched the world's first liquid fuel model rocket. This device, powered by gasoline and liquid oxygen, reached an altitude of 41 feet. It landed 2·5 seconds later and 184 feet away in a cabbage patch.

Goddard, as a boy, had read the works of Jules Verne and H. G. Wells. He had been dreaming, since then, of flying in space and of landing on the moon. The success of his preliminary experiments did not prevent him from being ridiculed by the press and, in 1929, from being forbidden by the State Fire Marshal to carry out any further model rocket launches in Massachusetts.

So, model rockets – the direct descendants of Dr. Goddard's visionary venture – are comparatively recent arrivals in the world of model aircraft. In every part of the United States, now, and in several other countries, model rockets of every shape and description are climbing into the sky line like their real-life counterparts at Cape Kennedy and Baikonur. These model rockets are built by men, women and young people who are participating in one of the fastest growing educational hobbies ever devised. Some modellers choose to build simple self-designed rockets. Others prefer to construct exact scale models of such famous launch vehicles as *Aerobee, Atlas, Delta, Nike, Saturn V* and *Titan*. Most are fiercely competitive.

Millions of model rockets are launched each year in the United States alone, but the safety record, in spite of all the keenness to win, is unparalleled. This happy state of affairs is due entirely to the efficiency of the officers of the National Association of Rocketry, America's controlling body. This association was brought into being, largely, to counter the wild enthusiasm of the earliest innovators who, in the years that immediately followed World War 2 and the V1 and V2 excitement, carried out numerous unscientific experiments with crude appliances that they called, hopefully, 'model rockets'. Usually, these 'rockets' were made from lengths of metal pipe or tube filled with some explosive mixture of the inventor's own compounding. Predictably, these crude adven-

his *skydart* model goes up under ower and then glides back to arth

188 Left – An exact scale model of the Saturn V rocket in flight

189 Two young rocketeers recover the two stages of a Saturn V model rocket returning to earth by parachute after a successful launch

tures ended all too often in disaster. Many limbs and eyes were lost when explosive charges were sparked off prematurely. A few accidents even proved fatal.

Now, all that has changed. 'During my years as Executive Director of the National Aeronautical Association I have watched the NAR (National Association of Rocketry) grow from a few members and a dozen sections into an organization of thousands of members and more than 130 sections', wrote Major General Brooke E. Allen, recently retired from the USAF. The founders of this association have laid down, from the start, strict safety regulations, and they have insisted that all their members conform to the code. Insurance cover is endangered if the rules are 'bent'.

First, they stipulate that model rockets shall only be powered with pre-loaded commercially produced engines. These engines

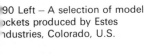

90 Left – A selection of model rockets produced by Estes Industries, Colorado, U.S.

91 Just like the real thing – an Estes Industries model rocket streaks off the launching pad and heads for the sky

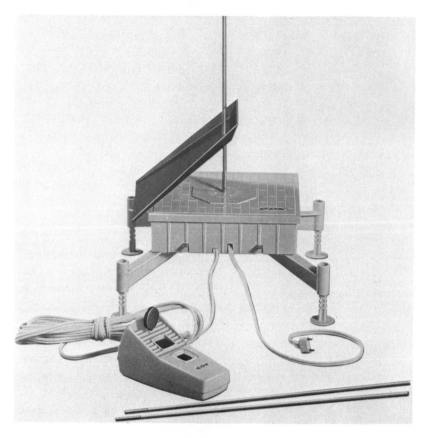

192 A model rocket launch system marketed by L. M. Cox Mfg Co., Inc. of California

193 Below – Centuri model rocket engines

are manufactured under carefully regulated conditions; they are made with solid fuel, and their behaviour is entirely predictable. They have taken the place – for all time, it is to be hoped – of the old hit-or-miss home made mixtures. No model rocket should weigh more than 453 grams (16 ounces) at lift-off, according to the NAR's present safety code, and none should contain more than 113 grams (4 ounces) of propellant. The Centuri Engineering Company of Phoenix, Arizona, based on a twenty-acre plant, is manufacturing more model rocket engine types as this book is being compiled than any other single undertaking in the world. As a special feature, Centuri engines have been formulated in such a way that they will emit high density smoke from their initial 'burnout', to make tracking easier.

In every instance, the NAR insists, these commercially-produced engines must be ignited by remotely-operated electrical firing systems. The use of matches and fuses, now, is out – this alone must have helped to prevent several fatal accidents. A simple igniting device may consist of a short piece of electrical resistance wire, bent so that it resembles an old-fashioned hairpin. A 6-volt battery, the poles of which are connected by longer wires to the ends of this 'hairpin', can supply the necessary power. At the last possible moment before take-off time, the curved mid-piece of the hairpin is moved into a shallow depression in the propellant. As soon as the operator is safely clear of the launching pad ('at least

94 A sophisticated model rocket launch control system introduced by Estes Industries

15 feet away from any rocket that is being launched') a master switch is thrown to complete the circuit. The switch should return automatically to the 'off' position when released.

As suitable materials for making model rockets, the officials of the NAR suggests lightweight materials such as paper, wood, plastic and rubber. They forbid the use of metal for the structural parts. ('What goes up, must come down' is one of the basic facts of life that model rocketeers forget at their peril – or at other people's. It is not very amusing to have a sizeable lump of aluminium or mild steel descend unexpectedly from the heavens on to one's unprotected cranium.) As commercially-produced model rocket engines are made to standardized dimensions, the inside diameters of model rocket body tubes have to be nicely gauged to accommodate them comfortably, with a suitably small clearance.

The NAR also recommend that every model rocket shall contain some recovery device which will return it gently to the ground so that it can be flown again. As a result of this requirement, many of the best model rockets today contain a neatly folded parachute, which is ejected by a charge in the engine that becomes effective only when all the lifting fuel has burned itself out. ('Seconds after lift off your Cox Model Rocket hits 1,800 feet', claims an advertisement put out by a well-known subsidiary of Leisure Dynamics, of Santa Ana, California. 'Then, the retro rocket pops the chute open, down it floats ready for another space shot. Model Rocketry is the most exciting new hobby in years. And now you can enjoy it minutes after leaving the store. . . . Get in on the excitement.') In some of the more sophisticated model rockets fitted with a device of this kind, a puff of smoke is emitted, high in the sky, just before the parachute is due to appear. This smoke signal, sent out by an innocuous delay charge, enables the operator on the ground far below to appreciate the full extent of his rocket's achievement. In-flight tracking of the A-20 *Demon* rocket, manufactured by Estes Industries, of Penrose, Colorado, is facilitated in another way – each rocket has a bright silver press-on trim that makes it highly visible in the sky.

The NAR, in formulating their code, did not forget the wide variety of angles at which a model rocket can be launched. If a rocket is allowed to travel too near the earth's surface, its progress may be deadly. So, the rule-makers insist that all launching devices shall be pointed within 30° of the vertical. (This ordinance has a useful side-effect: it ensures that a spent rocket will return to earth reasonably near the place from which it was launched and can, therefore, be recovered without too much difficulty.)

To assist the operator to find the occasional rocket that gets away, Estes Industries have developed a four-inch-long transmitter that will fit neatly into a standard body tube. Powered by a

195 Mike Dorffler, member of the Estes Industries research and development staff, places on the launch pad a two-stage *Omega* model rocket fitted with a movie camera. Mike devised this novel extension of model rocketry techniques.

196 A Centuri experimental model photographed just after lift off

197 Above — Two enthusiasts take the guesswork out of tracking with a model rocket altitude finder

198 Right — Safety first — observers keep a safe distance as a model rocket roars skywards

15-volt battery with a life of over twenty-four hours, this device sends out an intermittent bleep that can be picked up by an everyday walkie-talkie, or by a receiver set to a specified, unlicensed citizen band. The effective range of the Estes transmitter at the time of going to press is just over one mile. 'Used by itself, the TRANSROC is just the thing to help the rocketeer find his model in a patch of tall weeds', claims the President of the Estes Company confidently.

The full catalogue of rules governing model rocketry would only interest those directly concerned with this relatively specialized field, but a few more quotations from the NAR safety code may indicate some of the possibilities and limitations of this space age pastime:

I will not launch my model rocket in high winds, near buildings, power lines, tall trees, low flying aircraft or under any conditions which might be dangerous to people or property.

I will not launch rockets so that their flight path will carry them against targets on the ground, and will never use an explosive warhead nor a payload that is intended to be flammable.

I will never point a loaded rocket or its rocket nozzle at anyone,

199 Left — Model rockets ready for launch at the 1972 Transpo Airshow. The second model from the left has a parasite glider

200 Three Estes Industries plastic ready-to-fly model rockets. From left: the *Banshee*, the *Vampire* (or the Mini-pad Launch System), and the X-15

nor allow anyone to be in the flight path of a rocket during flight preparations.

There is no need for a very complicated structure to be provided for the controlled launch of a model rocket. Many operators manage with a length of $\frac{1}{8}$-inch diameter wire attached to a stable base. (Small guides, fixed to the body of the rocket, fit round the wire and ensure that the launch is made in the desired direction.) Other rocketeers, with a taste for gadgetry, prefer to construct launchers that resemble more nearly those seen at Cape Kennedy, the White Sands Proving Ground, or Wallops Island. Plastic, being virtually fireproof, is a popular material for these more ambitious appliances.

Sending up weight-lifting model rockets is a branch of the hobby that interests some of the more enterprising enthusiasts. Among the payloads that have been successfully carried by model rockets to considerable heights are still and light movie cameras, and they have brought back some very interesting pictures of the earth's surface. Tiny transmitters have been sent aloft, too – arranged, usually, to send down exact and up-to-the-second information of their rockets' altitude.

Flying model rockets in urban and suburban areas tends to be a sociable rather than a solitary occupation. An individual model rocketeer, trying to find a suitable flying field under these circum-

stances, is likely to find the venture difficult, unless he is lucky enough to know someone who happens to own one of the rare and valuable expanses of open ground that still exists in such places. A club or group of model rocketeers, on the other hand, is more likely to be granted the occasional use of a public park or school sports field, as long as there is a good public relations officer in attendance, who, by quoting the remarkable safety records of today's rocketeers, can gain the confidence of the authorities. So, competitive associations are formed, and area meets, regional meets and multi-state and national conventions fill up, in the United States and Canada, almost every available date in the calendar.

Britain, one of the countries in which model aircraft were principally pioneered, is at the time of writing unfriendly ground for model rocketeers. The two men in the team nominated to represent Britain in the first World Space Modellers' Championship held at Vrsac, Yugoslavia, in 1972 were told by Home Office officials that their 6-inch high rockets, which held up to four ounces of fuel, could be classified as explosives under the terms of the Explosives Act of 1875. Warned that he and his colleague risked a £100 fine if they practised lift-offs in Britain, Peter Freebrey, an expert who is technical secretary of the SMAE said that as he and his friend had worked for months on their four rockets, they still intended to compete. 'The first chance we will have to see whether our rockets really fly is at the championships,' he added. 'We are sure they will, and we hope to reach 1,000 feet. All the other countries sending teams have no trouble in practising. The Americans, who are very, very good, import their fuel from Scotland.'

The dreadful colds of deep winter that are experienced in the larger land masses of the Northern Hemisphere tend to discourage all but the hardiest of model rocketeers from working the whole year round. 'I have found that a frozen lake is an excellent launching field', wrote Tom Houghton, of Royal Oak, Michigan, to the Editor of *Model Rocketry*. 'There are no obstructions, and the white surface makes it easy to spot the recovered bird. So, winter is a perfect time for launching.' And, one model rocketeer in New Mexico, entering for the 'Winter Contest' promoted by the same magazine, managed a launch in a temperature of −17°.

But, Pittsburgh's Steel City Section of the American National Association of Rocketry has found that attendance at their cold weather meets has tended to drop practically to zero. One issue of *Starburst*, their newsletter, reported:

'There was a launch scheduled for December 20 at Hampton Field. Careful scientific observation has shown that the attend-

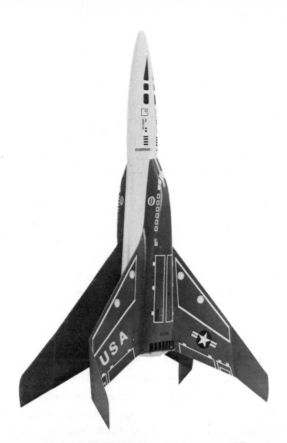

01 The Space Shuttle — a
manned re-usable space vehicle,
which is to be used for a wide
variety of missions in earth orbit,
s shown here as a Cox Mfg Co.
nc. model.

02 A NASA model of the Space
Shuttle shown in flight configuration with a large propellant
ank attached.

ance at our launches follows this equation, known as Crafton's Excuse Equation:

$$A = (T/W)\,S - V$$

This equation shows that the attendance (A) is proportional to the temperature (T). The colder it gets, the fewer people show up. Attendance is inversely proportional to the wind speed (W). It is also directly proportional to S, where S is the number of rockets Danny Sternglass has built in the last month. (He is one of the few members of the club who is actively building during the winter.) V is the quality of the television programming on the afternoon of the launch.

As an example of the use of this equation, let us calculate the attendance at the December launch. The temperature was about 25 degrees, the wind was 20 miles per hour. Danny had 3 new rockets, and there was a good football game, a bad movie, and a panel discussion on putting Christ back in Xmas on the television. Let's rate the TV at 1 for the football game, 0·5 for the old flick, and 0 for the panel show. Solving the equation yields a value of 2·25 for the attendance. I guess that panel show must have been worth a quarter of a point. Only two people showed up at the December launch . . .'

A light-hearted approach to the problems of model rocketry is not likely to be condemned outright by the authorities, many of whom feel that the competitive element in this branch of aero-modelling – already referred to, briefly – has gained, in recent years, a disproportionate importance. At times, claimed Chris Pocock in *Modroc Flyer*, newsletter of the South Seattle Rocket Society, keen rivalries have turned sour, leaving invisible scars in the rocketeers' minds. He enlarged:

'. . . Let us now consider the attitudes that prevail at a National meet, or any large gathering of eastern rocketeers. What do we see?

Rocketeers walk the range in battle dress complete with swords or knives. Threatening looks cover faces. Scale models are closely guarded and covered with plastic bags for protection from sabotage. Tempers are hot. Hostile remarks are made about plastics to the advocates of this old modeling material. Threats and plots are conceived and sometimes carried out . . .'

The best way to conquer the 'Kill, Maim and Destroy Syndrome' diagnosed so ably by Chris Pocock is, he suggests, to learn to take oneself less seriously and to smile even when one is losing. 'Let's put FUN back into model rocketry where it has all but vanished,' he concludes. 'Where it still flourishes, let's keep it!'

Above, a collection of old-time models at a rally.

Below, a large radio-controlled scale model with baby buggy wheels at Dayton, Ohio

14 Epilogue

It would be wrong and misleading to close this book on a sad note for, by and large, the aeromodelling fraternity is a very contented and co-operative one. At the FAI's Free Flight World Championships held at Säve in Sweden in 1971, for instance, members of the Russian team were giving away samples of their advanced towhook, Herbert Schmidt of Germany was discussing and demonstrating his technically brilliant model sailplane glider and, Christian Schwartzbach, a research engineer at the Technical University of Denmark at Copenhagen, where he supervises studies on turbulent jet flows, was advising other competitors about their airfoils and propellers (some of the best and most successful of which he had made for them!).

Above, The *Thinwall Special*, designed by Lou Roberts, is an -foot span power contest model; features two-piece wings.

Winner of the A/2 contest at the 1969 World Championships in Austria was the Englishman, Alton Drew (on the left); with him is the runner-up

03 A rubber-powered model of a Heinkel He 46 in flight. The engine cylinders were built up from balsa.

Let the last words come, then, from John Clemens, President in 1971 of the AMA. John was commenting on the Radio Control World Championships held in his own country, but his summation has an even wider significance:

204 No question about model aircraft being 'toys' with these huge Class D gas-powered models seen at a recent contest at Taft, California.

'. . . The declared reason for all of the effort and organization put into this world-wide competition was to establish the absolute champions in this particular phase of model flying. But I PEEPED BEHIND THE MASK and discovered the REAL REASON for international competitions of a sporting nature. The real reason is a tremendous desire on the part of all intelligent peoples to know one another, to understand one another, and to respect one another. The catalyst in this world-wide 'marriage' is to compete against each other at a conquerable problem level, in a friendly and understanding manner, and naked of all weapons except such an innocent device as a ball, a stopwatch, or perhaps a model airplane.

Thru sports we find jumping a hurdle, hitting a hockey puck or a ball, pole vaulting, driving a racing car, or perhaps FLYING A MODEL AIRPLANE has the *same* problems in *any language*. Suddenly we have a common meeting ground. We understand the other fellow's problems and even find ourselves being sympathetic with him. We know how his finger hurts when it is whacked by a propeller. We understand his heartbreak when the fruits of his modeling efforts are destroyed by a crash. We understand the smile and twinkle in his eye when a model plane performs as he really thought it should.

Why don't we have understanding in our other relationships, political, economic, and geographic?'

Glossary and Abbreviations

Actuator: A device fitted in a model aircraft enabling its controls to be moved by radio.

Aerodynamics: The study of the forces that act on a moving aircraft.

Airfoil (alternatively **Aerofoil):** The shape of the wing or lifting surface of an aircraft or model aircraft seen as a cross-section.

Airscrew: The propeller of an aircraft or model aircraft.

AMA: Academy of Model Aeronautics (USA).

Attack, Angle of: The angle at which the wing of an aircraft or model aircraft meets the air stream.

Augmenter Tube: A device used with a model aircraft's jet engine to increase its performance.

Autogiro: An aircraft which has freely rotating wings set above the fuselage.

Bellcrank: A device used in line-controlled model aircraft for operating the elevators and other moving parts.

Boost Glider: A model glider which is taken upwards by a rocket engine. The engine falls off when its fuel is spent.

Bulkhead: A transverse former used in the construction of an aircraft or model aircraft fuselage.

Camber: The curved shape of an aircraft's wing or tail plane from the leading edge to the trailing edge.

Carrier-wave System: An elementary form of radio control.

Centre of Gravity: The point round which an exactly balanced aircraft may be said to pivot.

Chassis: Sometimes used instead of landing gear.

Chord: The effective width of a wing or stabilizer surface.

Cockpit: That part of an aircraft or model aircraft that is designed to accommodate the pilot.

Combat Contest: A control-line contest in which the achievements of full-size military aircraft are emulated.

Control Handle: A device, held in the hand, from which the control lines lead to a model aircraft.

Control-line Flying: The operation of a tethered model aircraft, the movements of which can be regulated by the person holding the control line or lines.

Control Surface: A movable surface used for controlling the direction in which an aircraft, or model aircraft, is to travel.

Cowling: That part of an aircraft or model aircraft that is designed primarily as an engine cover.

Decal: A sheet transfer used to embellish a model aircraft. A shorter form of the word 'decalomania'.

Dethermalizer: A device fitted to a model aircraft which will cause it to lose height rapidly after a pre-determined interval of time.

Dihedral: The angle at which the wings of an aircraft or model aircraft are tilted, in relation to each other, in order to increase stability.

Dolly: A wheeled carriage, usually made of wire, from which fast line-controlled model aircraft may be launched.

Dope: A transparent adhesive usually made of nitrate, butyrate, or cellulose.

Drag: The resistance that an aircraft or model aircraft may experience as it passes through the air.

Elevator: Part of a horizontal tail plane or stabilizer that is hinged so that it can act as a control.

Escapement: An electro-mechanical device used to alter the controls of a radio-operated model aircraft.

FAI: Fédération Aéronautique Internationale (Europe).

Fillet: A component added to an aircraft or model aircraft where exterior surfaces meet. Its function is to provide a rounded contour so that wind resistance may be lowered.

Fin: The vertical tail surface of an aircraft or model aircraft. Usually, this is the name given to the immovable part of that surface. The hinged portion, used for controlling the direction in which the plane or model is travelling, is known as the rudder.

Flap: A component fixed by hinges to the trailing edge

of a model aircraft wing to make the model easier to control or to increase its potential drag.

Flash: An unrealistic roughness or protrusion that may be found on the surface of an injection-moulded plastic model.

Float: A buoyant component known sometimes as a 'pontoon' that helps to keep a rise-off-water aircraft afloat.

Flying Boat: A rise-off-water aircraft that has its fuselage shaped, as its name implies, like the hull of a boat.

Flying Scale Model: A miniature facsimile of a full-sized prototype plane that can be operated realistically.

Free Flight: A name given to the operation of model aircraft which are not controlled by radio or any form of line.

Fuselage: The name usually given to the body or main fore-and-aft member of an aircraft.

Galloping Ghost: An ingenious system of radio control that permits the rudder, elevator and engine throttle of a model aircraft to be operated simultaneously.

Gasoline: Alternative name for petrol.

Gassie: A model aircraft powered by an internal combustion engine.

G-Line Flying: A control-line system in which the model aircraft is tethered by a single cord or wire to the upper end of a short rod held in the operator's hand.

Glow Plug: A component with a heated wire element that may be used instead of a spark plug for igniting the fuel in a miniature internal-combustion engine.

Hand Launch (HL): Using the operator's hand to propel a model aircraft at the start of its flight.

Helicopter: An aircraft (or model) which is equipped with overhead power-driven rotor-blades that enable it to move in a vertical direction as well as in a horizontal plane.

HL: *see* Hand Launch.

HLG: Hand-launch glider.

Horn: A lever used in conjunction with a control surface.

Hydro model: A model aircraft designed to rise from, and descend to, a water surface.

Internal-combustion Engine: A form of engine much used in model aircraft in which the fuel is burned inside the cylinder.

Jig: A device specially designed for holding together the component parts of a prototype or of a model while they are being assembled.

Kit: A collection of parts from which a model can be assembled.

Landing Gear (Undercarriage): The arrangement of struts and wheels on which an aircraft or model aircraft rests when it is stationary, and which supports it on take-off and landing.

Leading Edge: The front edge of a wing or tail surface.

Lift: Vertical force that supports an aircraft or model aircraft in flight, overcoming gravity.

Lift Coefficient: A figure that represents the relative efficiency of an airfoil section.

Longerons: The principal fore-and-aft members of an aircraft or model aircraft fuselage.

Lubricant: A fluid with which the strands of the rubber engine of a model aircraft may be treated, to improve its performance or to prolong its working life.

MAAC: Model Aeronautics Association of Canada.

Microfilm: An extremely thin transparent sheet made by floating some specially compounded fluid over a water surface, and used, when it has taken its permanent form, as an ultra-light covering for model aircraft.

Mono-line: Control-line flying of a relatively simple kind in which one line only is used, being twisted to alter the trim of the elevators of a model aircraft.

Muffler: A device intended to lessen the noise generated by a model aircraft engine.

NAA: National Aeronautic Association (USA).

NAR: National Association of Rocketry (USA).

NFFS: National Free Flight Society (USA).

Ornithopter: A primitive flying device, intended to move forwards by flapping its wings, as a bird does.

Payload: The freight carried by a model aircraft in a contest for transport planes.

Petrol: Alternative name for gasoline.

Pitch: A theoretical figure representing the distance that a propeller should travel forward with each revolution.

Pitot Tube: A tube projecting from an aircraft or model aircraft. In the prototype used in assessing the air-speed.

Polyhedral: A sophisticated form of dihedral in which the wing is constructed from a number of adjoining surfaces, each of which is inclined upwards at a different angle.

Pontoon: *see* Float.

Propeller: An airscrew used to push or pull a full-sized aircraft or a model plane.

Proportional: A radio-control system in which the movement of a pivoted rod, or rods, on the transmitter produces an equivalent effect on the control surfaces of the model.

Pull Test: A test that a control-line model aircraft must undergo before it takes part in any competition to make sure that it is safely tethered and not a potential danger.

Pulse Proportional: A radio-control system in which the control surfaces of the model may be seen to flutter continuously, like the wings of a moth.

Pusher: An aircraft (or model) that has its source of power mounted ahead of its propeller.

Pylon: A support used for a model aircraft's wing where that wing is to be raised above the fuselage.

Pylon Racing: The racing of radio-controlled model aircraft round a course marked out at the corners with pylons.

Quench Coil: A component of early radio-control apparatus.

Rat Racing: A form of control-line contest that is not subject to excessive regulations.

Resistance: The readiness or unreadiness of the air to part as an aircraft or model aircraft moves forward.

Reynolds' Number: A theoretical figure that indicates the difference between the performance of a model aircraft's wing and that of the wing of the full-sized prototype.

R/C: Radio-control.

Rise-off-Ground (ROG): A model aircraft that will become airborne, from a flat firm surface, under its own power.

Rise-off-Water (ROW): A model aircraft that will become airborne, from a water surface, under its own power.

Riser: An ascending current of air that will carry a model aircraft upwards (see also Thermal).

ROG: *see* Rise-off-Ground.

ROW: *see* Rise-off-Water.

RTP: Round-the-Pole.

Rudder: A vertical surface, or part of one, situated normally at the rear of an aircraft. To qualify for the name 'rudder', as opposed to 'fin', the surface must be movable so that it can be used for turning the plane to right or left.

Sail Plane: An exceptionally mobile glider which can travel for long distances in suitable rising air currents.

Servo: A mechanical device which alters the controls of a model aircraft in accordance with radioed 'instructions'.

Shut-off: A device which seals off the supply of fuel to the engine or engines of a model aircraft after a given interval of time so that the duration of its powered flight may be strictly controlled.

Slip Stream: The air moved in a rearward direction by the rotating propeller.

SMAE: Society of Model Aeronautical Engineers (Great Britain).

Spar: A structurally important member set spanwise in the wing or tail of an aircraft or model aircraft.

Sponson: A rudimentary wing projecting from the hull of a flying boat or model flying boat that helps (with its counterpart on the opposite side of the hull) to provide stability.

Stability: The tendency of an aircraft or model aircraft to fly on a level course in spite of any hazards that may happen to upset it.

Stabilizer (or 'Stab'): A horizontal surface, fixed at the rear of an aircraft or model aircraft, that helps to keep that aircraft stable.

Stall: A serious and possibly disastrous loss of lift suffered by an aircraft or model aircraft.

Step: A sudden change of level in the under-surface of the hull or floats of a hydroplane or model hydroplane which, by reducing suction, will help that craft to become airborne.

Stick Model: A model aircraft which has a single straight member acting as its fuselage.

Streamline: The most efficient shape that can be found for a solid body (such as a model aircraft) which has to pass rapidly through the air.

Stretch-winding: An effective method, invented in the U.S.A., of winding a rubber motor.

Stringer: A light, thin member used to support the outer skin of a fuselage.

Superhet: A short form of Superheterodyne. A relatively sophisticated type of receiver used in radio-control flying.

Super-Regen: A short form of Super-regenerative. Frequently abbreviated still further to 'Regen'. A less sophisticated type of receiver used in radio-control flying.

Tab: A small hinged surface on the wing or tail of an aircraft or model aircraft that can be used to adjust the trim of that plane or model.

Tail: The plane surfaces found normally at the rear end of an aircraft (or model aircraft) fuselage.

Tail Skid: A member, projecting downwards from the fuselage, that supports the rear end of an aircraft (or model aircraft) while it is on the ground and helps to keep it intact while the plane takes off and lands.

Team racer: A control-line model aircraft that conforms to certain fairly precise specifications and which is flown competitively against similar models.

Thermal: An ascending current of relatively warm air.

Thinner: A fluid used for diluting a model-maker's dope or cement.

Thrust: The forward-driving force generated by the engine/s, or revolving propeller of an aircraft or model aircraft.

Thrust Bearing: A component fitted to the nose of a model aircraft to house the propeller shaft, or to protect the fuselage from an undue amount of thrust produced by the propeller.

Tone System: A more advanced form of radio control than the carrier-wave system.

Torque: The force produced by a swiftly revolving propeller that tends to turn a model aircraft off a straight and level course.

Towline: A string or cord used for pulling a model glider or sailplane until it becomes independently airborne.

Tractor: A pulling airscrew or a model aircraft equipped with such a propeller.

Trailing Edge: The aft edge of an aircraft's (or model aircraft's) wing or tail surface.

Transmitter: A device used for sending radio signals to a model aircraft.

Trimotor: An aircraft or model aircraft with three motors.

U-Control: The original American name for control-line flight.

Undercarriage: *see* Landing Gear.

Variable Pitch: An airscrew made in such a way that all points along the blade will (in theory) travel the same distance forward in a revolution.

Windscreen (Windshield): A transparent surface used to protect a pilot or crew member.

For Further Reading

Bowden, Lt-Col C. E. *The History and Technical Development of Model Aircraft*. The Harborough Publishing Co., Leicester, 1946

Chinn, P. G. F. *All About Model Aircraft*. Model and Allied Publications, Hemel Hempstead, 1968

Dean, Bill. *Bill Dean's Book of Balsa Models*. Arco Publications, New York, Revised Edition 1970

Gilmore, H. H. *Model Planes for Beginners*. Harper and Row, New York, Revised Edition 1957

Hertz, Louis H. *Complete Book of Model Aircraft, Spacecraft and Rockets*. Crown, New York, 1967

Laumer, Keith. *How to Design and Build Flying Models*. Harper and Row, New York, Revised Edition 1970

Lopshire Robert. *Beginner's Guide to Building and Flying Model Airplanes*. Harper and Row, New York, 1967

McEntee, H. G. *Getting Started in R/C*. Potomac Aviation Publications, Washington, D.C., 1968

McEntee, H. G. *The Model Aircraft Handbook*. Thomas Y. Crowell, New York, 1968; Robert Hale, London, 1970

Malkin, J. *Aerofoil Sections*. J. Malkin, Upper Hutt, New Zealand

Mottin, H. C. *Getting Started in Control-Line*. Potomac Aviation Publications, Washington, D.C., 1969

Moulton, R. G. *Control Line Manual*. Model and Allied Publications, Hemel Hempstead, 1969

Moulton, R. G. *Flying Scale Models*. Model and Allied Publications, Hemel Hempstead, 1956

Moulton, R. G. *Model Aero Engine Encyclopedia*. Model and Allied Publications, Hemel Hempstead, 1969

Musciano, Walter A. *Building and Flying Model Airplanes*. Funk and Wagnalls, New York, 1971

Warring, R. H. *Multichannel Radio Control*. Model and Allied Publications, Hemel Hempstead, 1966

Warring, R. H. *Single Channel Radio Control*. Model and Allied Publications, Hemel Hempstead, 1967

List of Illustrations

BLACK AND WHITE

ndex

Figures in italics refer to pages on which some relevant illustrations may be found